Good Things Happen in the Dark

"Ellen Compton's prose is a rare and unique delight. Her zest for life and passion for understanding all that surrounds us (as well as all that is within us) will surprise and inspire you in equal measure. Thought-provoking, profoundly smart, and consistently entertaining. If you are looking for insight in your life, be sure to devour Ellen Compton's new book."

JAMES MULLINGER
Award-Winning Comedian, Writer, Editor-in-Chief of *Maritime Edit* magazine

"Ellen's collection is as beautifully crafted as a rosary, each essay a gem to carry in one's pocket, to rub between thumb and index as a mudra, a symbolic gesture invoking the holy inside each ordinary moment. Her honest, incisive, and often humorous incursion into her own life and story invites us to look with equal tenderness upon our own her(his)stories, to consider the sacredness of the body as elemental and viscerally connected to all created things. To fully inhabit our interiority with curiosity and honor, so that we might belong firstly to ourselves and then to each other."

DR. SIMONA CHITESCU WEIK
Poet, Teacher, Spiritual Companion, and Embodiment Practitioner

"No questions about it, put this book in your cart, and then hold onto your flippin' hat. This excellent, hilarious, and raw read equips you to give the those societal pressures that make you feel 'less than' a big, kind, Canadian punch in the face! (Think Jen Hatmaker in a badass biker gang, and you've got Ellen Compton). Rarely do words in our content-crammed days read as though they were picked with such care and finesse as they do in *Good Things Happen in the Dark*. Ellen is *truly* a linguistic Goddess whose indomitable frequency will turn the spirituality/self-care industry on its head."

MEGGIE LEE CALVIN
Bestselling Author of *I Am My Own Sanctuary: How A Recovering Holy-Roller Found Healing and Power*

"Ellen and I go way back, and she has always impressed me as a courageously independent and free person. I've witnessed this offend some. But I've also watched this inspire others. Including me! What is so marvelous is that her courage, independence, and freedom get to blend in this book with her desire to inspire you. I was happy when I first read it to hear her voice and see her authentic self expressed through the pages. I especially like the 'get real' parts. I believe this is her special contribution to the world. I really do think it will indeed inspire you."

DAVID HAYWARD
aka 'nakedpastor'

"*Good Things Happen in the Dark* is like taking a road trip with your big sister, including all the inside jokes, gentle commiseration, and tough love advice that comes with growing up and into your unique self. Ellen knows how to wrangle the stream of consciousness into a series of metaphors and analogies that connects life experiences with Divine intervention. Reading this in my 40s (and during a self-proclaimed mid-life crisis) is like relearning who I am, putting my 'spiritual glasses' on and seeing my Wonder Woman self, 'complete with cuffs and crown.'"

ANNA RHEA
Owner of Joppa Editing

Good Things Happen in the Dark

---

*A Candid Manifesto for
Courageous Authenticity*

Ellen Compton

Cover design and layout by Rafael Polendo (polendo.net)
Cover image by Storyblocks.com

First Edition

ISBN 978-1-938480-92-8

 QUOIR

Published by Quoir
Oak Glen, California
www.quoir.com

Dedication

For Cohen and Ingrid.
For anyone who has ever felt like too much and not enough.
For all the hard things that attempted to take me out. Nice try.

Contents

Introduction

Hey, Friend!

I'm so glad you're here. In choosing this book, I already know you're my cup of tea—one who wants to live fully and intrepidly. One who has determined to dive deeply. One who spurns the game of fitting in. You may be a spiritual anarchist, a person of faith, and likely, both at the same time. Perhaps you're also craving authenticity, and, hopefully, courage. Because, if we're honest, you can't have authenticity sans courage.

Many organizations, religious institutions, and individuals throw around buzz words like *authenticity,* claiming to encourage it. Claiming it's a core value. Claiming the *real you* is welcome here. But it's bullshit. It might be encouraged, but often, it's also punished, corrected, and sanitized.

Living an authentic life can look like an act of rebellion; an iconoclastic way of engaging that refuses modus operandi. Living with authenticity means being fully you. All the time. It is embracing the *intended you* before life experiences, trends, norms, religious rules, and social pressures attempted to make you more, make you less, water down your spicy, file your edges, or put you in a back room where you wouldn't bore or offend.

Things are not as they appear. Much of life has been categorized into good and bad, wins and losses, success and failure, light and dark, sacred and secular. But the more we learn, the more we know it *isn't* one or the other. Living in a way that is richly authentic means acknowledging and courageously holding in tension the apparent binaries that make up this life.

Everything belongs. Everything has purpose. Everything has meaning.

Thematically, overlap exists between the chapters in this book. I have attempted to assign them to sections in a way that makes sense; however, as mentioned above, things rarely fit into one category, and the same is true here. If we have met before, whether in person or in writing, you've likely ascertained that I understand all of life in metaphors and pictures. Analogies are how I make sense of the world. My brain searches for and assigns meaning to every single situation (the jury is still out on whether this makes me super weird or super awesome).

Though I had thought to begin with a formal introduction, I quickly realized the redundancy of such a choice, for, by nature, I am quite meta—that is self-referential. By the end of this journey together, you will be well-acquainted with an abundance of odd and unique (and sometimes embarrassing) facts about me. More than this, my hope is that you will be well-acquainted and deeply in love with every odd and unique aspect of yourself—your real, unabridged, perfectly-loved self.

Much love to you.

Ellen

Prologue

Naked and Afraid

"Honor the space between no longer and not yet."
NANCY LEVIN

D o you want to go on a journey? It won't be comfortable, but growth rarely is. As much as we would love to avoid the discomfort of transition, we recognize that there is purpose in the process. Growing pains are aptly named. The aching means something is happening.

Hermit crabs exemplify an intriguing metaphor. By nature of their aquatic group, *crustacea*, one could assume these beings carry their permanent protective coverings at all times. But this is not true. These soft-bellied creatures take up residence in the discarded shells of other creatures. A hermit crab will inhabit its shell until it has grown to the point of discomfort, and it is no longer feasible to stay without consequence. To linger in the current shell means the crab's growth will be inhibited; no longer able to protect itself by withdrawing fully into its armor. What *was* a protective abode, right for the season, has become a growth-limiting, tight space.

At this point, it must decide: stay or go.

It would be folly to remain in the current shell, but the other option is to begin a dangerous voyage between point A and point B. Transition.

Ideally, the crab has its eyes set on the next shell it will inhabit, but this is not always the case, and even when it is, there is inherent risk. The hermit crab must endure a season of significant vulnerability as it leaves the 'too small' shell in search of its next dwelling.

How many times have I felt like a hermit crab, somewhere between point A and point B? These are the phases of life when it has become obvious that I can no longer stay in my current situation, but the next step remains hidden from me. This state of limbo, teetering on the precipice of change, is daunting. If I leave the safe confines of what I know in search of what is next, I risk exposure and vulnerability. Who knows how long the journey will even take? My soft, shell-less body will be unprotected and open to all kinds of attacks.

I contemplate whether or not it would be better to stay put, but honestly, this option, though seemingly less perilous, doesn't work either. I have developed beyond what this current place can offer or protect; it no longer fits. And so, like the hermit crab, I have to decide whether to stay safe and stop growing, or embrace vulnerability and grow.

For most of us, willful discomfort isn't something we seek, but we also know that growth does not occur in the comfort zone. Shunning growth equates to turning away from becoming who we were created to be. And so, with gritted teeth, I will continue to choose growth over comfort.

My transition journeys often begin with positivity and determination. Though I may or may not have a sense of what is next, I begin with hope and lean hard on faith. This feeling of adventure and 'whatever it takes' usually sustains me for a while. I do my best not to have concrete ideas about what it all means and how it will play out.

Yet, my personality is such that there is usually a very detailed map lurking somewhere just beneath my consciousness. "Laid back" is not a descriptor that has *ever* been used for me, though I *am* learning to allow life to unfold.

When the vulnerable journey between shells takes longer than anticipated, which it inevitably does, there are a couple of traps I have learned to identify, only by nature of having fallen into them repeatedly.

There have been times—*a lot* of times—that I have longed to return to a metaphorical captor. At least in captivity, I knew the rules! I may have been a slave and it might have been subsistence living, but I knew what to expect and could *make do* with what was, even if it wasn't always enough. My temptation partway into a journey can be to return to what I knew, to the known and the comfortable, even if it wasn't right. Steeling myself to resist the urge, I continue moving forward.

A second stumbling block I often encounter in the interim is the temptation to settle. There are times when I've been annoyed with God because it seemed that we were journeying past perfectly good shells. "This is actually *good enough*. Let's stop here. I'll be content with this!" The lure of the *good enough* is almost stronger than the lure of 'what was.' The adage "the good is the enemy of the best" is certainly what's at play here. Though these shells would function, they are not the end goal. Not the best.

Transition is not random, meaningless discomfort, but a purposeful plan that will certainly come and not delay. And so, let's allow it to unfold. Lean in and trust that Love will hold you safe. Let's embrace the vulnerability; the feelings of being unmoored, homeless, naked, and exposed without our protective shells.

I promise you, it will be worth it. Are you ready?

Unguarded

(My Dark and Twisty Self)

Chapter 1

Good Things Happen in the Dark

"Sometimes when you're in a dark place, you think you've been buried, but actually you've been planted."

CHRISTINE CAINE

Many of us dread the darkness. It shelters the monster under the bed, the boogie man, evil, and all things nefarious. Darkness must be avoided. We push it away by any means necessary—quelling, numbing, pretending. We deem it *bad* and fight with all of our might to keep the lights on.

I have been in great darkness. Actually, allow me to be more honest. I *am* in great darkness. Most of the time, you would never know it to see me. I choose joy. I fix my eyes on goodness. I cling to hope. I engage in loving kindness. I try to be careful with my words. But it's all taken an extreme amount of determination.

There's a significant difference between talking transparently about where we *have been* once we're on the other side of it, and talking vulnerably from where *we are*.

Vulnerably, I'm coming to you from my darkness; a darkness that has been constructed layer by layer by layer over this last while. Layers of disappointment, heartbreak, fear, disgust—with individual people, with groups, with institutions, and with the world at large.

At first, with only one layer, I was like a child under a blanket, covered, but still able to discern shapes and light. With another layer, the forms of things began to disappear, though I was still able to identify sources of brightness. Another layer removed sight and light. Another layer made it too warm and muffled. Another layer rendered it difficult to breathe. Another layer paralyzed me. And now, it sometimes feels like you can no longer see me. And I can no longer see you. This is where I've been. *This is where I am.*

But what if darkness has been villainized? What if we look at darkness differently?

We *always* have a choice. We can resist the darkness, cowering and suffering, avoiding and reviling.

Or we can embrace it.

Because, my friends, many exceptional and meaningful things happen in the dark.

Sometimes the darkness is frightening. Sometimes the lights do need to be turned on to expose the tiny, lurking fears that have been harassing us. But often the darkness is rich and important. We need to *leave it be* if we desire the fullness and growth that is intended for us.

Though I likely wouldn't be the first to volunteer for a dark season (*"Pick me! Pick me!"*), I *will* be the first to acknowledge that most of my character growth has occurred in the dark.

Darkness is essential during gestation. New humans and animals grow inside the safe, nurturing darkness of their mothers' wombs.

Darkness is imperative for the development of fine art photography. An invasion of light obscures what should have been clear and defined.

Darkness is necessary for a good night's sleep. Total darkness increases the body's production of melatonin. And it is during this sleep that our minds regroup, and our bodies heal and grow.

Darkness is intimate. A close sharing of space, of air, of proximity. Lovers reaching for one another in the night.

Darkness is a vital part of transformation. A caterpillar in chrysalis form must be wrapped up and protected for the miracle to occur. Interestingly, synonyms for this dark little cocoon include evolution, expansion, improvement, increase, maturity, advancement, and development.

Darkness is imperative for the sprouting of seeds. Those exposed to direct light dry out and die. But those that are forced into the darkness of the ground produce life.

So I am embracing the darkness. I am reframing the darkness. I am not going to be bitter. I am not going to rot in the ground. I am not going to disappear.

Instead of feeling lost and afraid, I will choose hidden and safe. Instead of feeling disorientated and vulnerable, I will choose held and comforted in the shadow of the wing. Instead of feeling buried alive, I will choose *planted.*

We can't rush the process. We need to resist the urge to brush back the soil to see what's happening. Do not subvert germination by digging up the seed. Stop checking up. Stop checking in.

During this season, I'm waiting quietly and safely in the darkness. I'm allowing my tears to flow as often as needed; these tears water the soil that nurtures the seed.

It will seem like nothing is happening. It will feel like you are dead in the ground. But if you wait, you'll crack open and roots will begin to grow. Above ground, you and others might observe that nothing is happening, but your roots *need* to push down deep in order to sustain any life that will appear on the surface. Then suddenly, it will happen.

Green sprouts will emerge, and the life that has been forming in the dark will be visible to you, and to others.

But the dark part has to happen first.

In the meantime, you are safe. You are held. You are growing. You are going to thrive. And so am I.

Good things happen in the dark.

Chapter 2

Opting for Uncomfortable

*"Anything I've ever done that was ultimately
worthwhile initially scared me to death."*
ANONYMOUS

A few weeks ago, I found myself in a situation that located my heart firmly in my throat. As I stood behind a piano on a stage for the first time in years, I wondered what the heck I had done? How could I *possibly* have agreed to this? Leading music from piano *used* to feel completely comfortable for me, but after five years of leading only with my voice, this no longer felt okay. In fact, my brain was interpreting it as the *exact opposite* of okay. It might as well have been a saber-tooth tiger crouching for attack. Or a Junebug.

During rehearsal, feeling entirely overwhelmed and very much in-over-my-head, this fully-grown, mature person actually contemplated *faking sick* and running out of the building.

And then a counterintuitive thought began forming in my mind: *"What if this is good for me?"*

My response? *"Oh no you don't, brain. You don't get to re-frame this horrid situation into something useful!"*

Like most people, I prefer to be good at things. I desire to do things well. I gravitate toward situations where I feel confident, in my *wheelhouse,* and capable. While this *sounds* entirely reasonable, if we are not careful, we can easily begin to live small, fearful of failure, and avoidant of opportunities that call us away from our field of expertise and into the realm of average.

"There's no growth in the comfort zone and no comfort in the growth zone." [1] *(Anonymous)*

This favored quote of mine has recently come back to bite me. Previously, I'd applied it almost exclusively to personal growth, inner healing, and ideas pertaining to identity. But I've begun to recognize that it applies, also, to intentionally opening ourselves to experiences that aren't a *sure thing* in terms of success—like playing sub-par piano in a venue full of people.

There are seasons in life when it's wise to seek and accept comfort. And, there are seasons for growth when it's essential for your overall well-being to put yourself out there, to leave the realm of exceptional and be completely *mediocre* for a while ... or even straight-up *awful.*

Your brain might fight you on this, but the truth is, it's healthy to step outside of our comfort zones, to try something new, to go back to beginner. Maybe this looks like engaging a hobby you haven't explored in a long time. Maybe it means signing up for a Spanish course. Maybe it means being brave with your words, knowing they will rock the boat. Maybe it looks like auditioning for a part in a musical, or joining a sports team. Maybe it means leaving a successful career to pursue a dream.

This past year, awakened to the call of adventure, I sought change. For almost two decades, I worked as an elementary school teacher in the same school. I knew my colleagues. I knew the rules. I knew the norms. I knew the larger school community. I knew the families. I knew where the art supplies were stored. I knew who had extra coffee pods when I ran out. I knew the best times to photocopy in order to avoid waiting. I knew that my administration (my bosses) supported me and my *sometimes* wildly-off-roading-brain children. I felt trusted. They knew I worked hard and cared deeply for my kids each year, and I didn't have to prove myself. My classroom felt like a second home.

So why in the world would I decide to leave the known for the unknown? Why leave expert behind? Why opt for uncomfortable?

Because I want to stay awake. While it's comforting to know the ropes and to be the expert, when we've done the same thing for a long time, the 'challenging' becomes the 'mundane.' When we are *accustomed* to the point that things no longer require our rapt attention, we can become blind; we fall asleep. Though I have such affection for my now 'former' school and colleagues, I had a longing for what was beyond the shore. (Moana, I get you. Totally.) I have an intense desire to keep growing and learning. To pay attention. Going back to beginner helps us to see again. To appreciate the details. To stay awake in our lives.

Because I want freedom from fear. Upon hearing my decision to embrace a new adventure, *many* people asked, "But what about your pension?" and other such practical questions. When we rely on circumstances and structures for our safety—whether financial, social, or otherwise—the idea of leaving those comfort zones can make us fearful. If we make ourselves beholden to the known, we become slaves to it. Engaging change— trusting that our needs will be met and that we can successfully navigate the transitions—allows us to step out of fear. To be clear, I'm as careful and rigid as they come when it comes to finances and responsibilities, so I'm not advocating leaping blindly. It's only smart to check your gear before launching yourself over the edge. But then ... launch yourself over the edge! Trust the process even if it feels like free-fall for a bit. Step out and leave fear in the rear-view mirror.

Because I Want A Strong Brain. Left to their own devices, our brains are lazy. Once they build pathways and make necessary connections, they typically settle into auto-pilot. It no longer takes any thought to complete a task. Think about driving a familiar route—it's possible to get there and not even remember driving because our brains know exactly where we are going.

Our brains are also risk-averse. In my classroom, you'll often hear me saying, *"If you're not making mistakes, you're not risking. If you're not risking, you're not growing."* I share frequently with my students that grades are not necessarily an indication of hard work. Effort counts for so much! In my opinion, an average "C" that has cost something in terms of effort, risk, hard work, perseverance, and courage is far more valuable than something that was easy. Sure, we love to see a report card of "straight As," but if those were easy As that came with little to no effort, then suddenly, they look a little more brassy and a lot less gold.

In order to continue growing and strengthening our brains, we have to do things differently. Take a different road home. Brush our teeth with the opposite hand. Try something new. As much as we might think we like comfort, our brains need and ultimately *appreciate* being forced to work.

Because I want to say *yes* to the call. Some people might refer to it as "the writing on the wall." Some might call it guidance. For me, it's usually the voice of the divine. No, not an audible, booming Charlton Heston/God voice, but that still, small voice inside me. That voice that *could* be mistaken for my own thoughts, except the thoughts carry a different kind of weight. A kindness and an exhortation. An impact far greater than my own meandering thoughts. This is what propelled my decision toward a new adventure.

More than a year ago, I sensed that something would be shifting, that it was time for a change. I pursued various leads that seemed good to me, but in the end, they were not the thing. And then I stumbled on to a particular school website that nearly took my breath away. The mission statement and core values mirrored my own. The educational philosophy sounded like *me*. I recognized in an instant that this was *the thing*. And so I waited. I checked the career opportunities page regularly as I waited for my future job to be posted. The process was rigorous *and* filled with ease all at once. As each new door appeared before me, I simply walked through it.

While I have a thousand years of teaching experience and 'know' many facts about my new educational home, I would also be navigating lots of unknowns—older students, new colleagues, distinct norms and mores. At this point, I hardly know where the light switch is in my own classroom! But still, I *know in my knower* that this change is right and necessary. And though I'll feel like a beginner for a little while, all of the unknowns will soon become known.

Though seemingly paradoxical, to live fully and richly, there are times when we have to step outside of our comfort zones. Nope, it's not comfortable. But it needs to be done.

Chapter 3

Holding On for Dear Life!

"Hope is not about proving anything. It's about choosing to believe this one thing, that love is bigger than any grim, bleak shit anyone can throw at us."

ANNE LAMOTT

Life is gorgeous, and hard, and awe-inspiring, and messy. We can re-frame, see *all* the silver linings, count it as blessing in disguise, speak positively, and practice gratitude. We can and we should and we *do*. But this doesn't negate the existence of painful things.

Yes, life is wondrous, and it can still be hard.

Perhaps you'll be tempted to tag me as *pessimistic* or *void of faith*, but before you do, how about reaching, instead, for the word *honest*? I feel called to shout *truth from the trenches* of life, to live vulnerably and authentically, to voice what most of us feel.

There are some very real struggles *around* us and *in* us. And I'm not sure why this truth tends to throw us off-kilter because in God's book, we're actually given a heads up that *we will* have trouble in this world.[1]

In terms of perception of safety, there seems to be a natural progression for most humans. These are massive, sweeping, simplified generalizations, but the point is to show development through life stages.

Early on, so long as a baby's needs are met—warm, clean, fed, and comforted—the baby will feel safe. In later months, a baby or young child may experience anxiety when separated from the adult to whom he, she or they is attached but will soon learn that while adults may leave, they will surely return. In a healthy attachment situation, a child will launch into the world, feeling capable and mostly free from fear. As an adolescent, the experience of safety and immunity to consequence becomes even stronger, as the brain rewires and the prefrontal cortex (the part that insists on self-control and well-thought out plans) temporarily abdicates its position. (As a parent of teenagers, this is terrifying). Eventually, we experience a few hard knocks to help us understand that we are not invincible. Not strong. Not above the natural consequences of our choices. Not immune to pain.

For me, the deconstruction of my perceived safety began as a young teenager and continued intermittently into my thirties.

Romantic notions like "marriage lasts forever" were countered with reality when my own parents' marriage ended. And then later, my own. Suddenly, that covenant which had seemed inalterable to me was vulnerable. I was dismayed to understand it was a fragile entity, not insusceptible to real life. It changed my view of true love from *trusting belief* to *how do you know?* Blunt truth: you really don't.

The *fame*-like ideal, *"I'm gonna live forever!"*, came crashing down when I was sixteen years old. As a pastor's kid, I'd been around death my entire life. By the time I was ten years old, I'm sure I visited more funeral homes with my dad than most people do in a lifetime. But these were old people. Their turn was over. When I was in tenth grade, one of my best friends was killed in a car accident. She was fifteen. There was no foul play, no alcohol. Only bad road conditions, inexperienced driving, and an inflated sense of safety. On that day, just before Christmas, I got a phone call from a hysterical little sister telling me that my friend and two others were gone. It's amazing how the tears still come when I revisit this now decade's old memory. I remember recognizing that life as I knew it was forever altered. I understood that we are not safe and that we are not guaranteed immunity from death.

Another myth dispelled in my early-twenties was the *romantic comedy film plot*: my person and I would meet, something hard would happen to separate us or to blind us to our love, but in the end, it would all work out. Happily ever after. At nineteen years old, I met someone who I was confident I would marry (thank you, Evangelical indoctrination). We were friends, but I loved him more than that. Although he didn't recognize it as more, I was certain he would eventually know we were meant to be. My heart was *betrothed* to him for years, unbeknownst to him. Years later, only days after I finally found the courage to send him an honest letter, I learned through a friend that he had just got engaged. My letter was already in the mail. Heartbreak and humiliation. And then he got married. End of dream. Thanks for the letdown, Hallmark.

In my early twenties, I experienced a friendship that was rich and life-giving. I had never been more open and accountable. I felt so safe and loved. I shared myself deeply, only to learn later that my confidences hadn't been respected or treasured. My faith and safety in friendship was rocked.

Suicide is another realm that remained blissfully inconsequential until it infiltrated the realm of possible. Though I knew of people who'd committed suicide, it wasn't something I thought much about or even entertained as possible. It was *not in my backyard*. When someone important to my family took his own life, it revealed a door that had previously not existed. *Before*, when someone wasn't answering my phone call, the reason was clearly that they had forgotten to charge their phone or they were sleeping. *After,* my first thoughts in every scenario flew to suicide. I realized fearfully and heartbreakingly that humans are so very vulnerable.

All of these hardships curbed the reckless safety in which I'd lived. These realities burst through the false walls of immunity that I'd so carefully constructed. They introduced plot lines that I'd never intended for my life. I was going to grow up, be very educated, be a rockstar, fall in love, get married forever, have lots of children, and hugely impact the world. There would be no rejection, no broken trust, no divorce, no death. So when all of these things were introduced into my experience, my world was shaken. I realized with despair that I wasn't really safe.

This tight space, almost like a bottle neck or funnel, occurs for all of us at some point. The revelation can cause a number of responses. In my life, the option that presented was the choice between despair and fear *or* hoping in something or someone higher. For me, it was the someone higher. Hoping in God became the pathway to a new kind of safety. Not in myself, but in Love.

Finding our security in God doesn't mean that we now wear some sort of supernatural immunity cloak. We live in a world that is broken and the rain falls justly and unjustly. The difference is in our *experience* of the hard things. We are promised over and over that God is with us.

A life of faith doesn't make us exempt from adversity. Those who hope for only health and wealth will surely be disappointed. I believe God *is* good—the source of hope, joy, peace, fulfillment, identity, comfort, wisdom and healing—but it doesn't always feel like that. We are not promised problem-free living. Because we live in this beautiful but imperfect world, we *do* experience challenges like sickness, death, betrayal, and loneliness.

While we may not always feel bubble-wrapped or be plucked from terrible situations like we'd wished, what we *do* have is *God with us.* We are not alone in the hard things. We are strengthened and held together. All things can be repurposed for our ultimate good. Even the parts that don't make sense, like the earthquakes that rock our foundations.

One of my favorite (and possibly most-prayed) pieces of writing is this excerpt from "Saint Patrick's Breastplate":

Christ with me,
Christ before me,
Christ behind me,
Christ in me,
Christ beneath me,
Christ above me,
Christ on my right,
Christ on my left,
Christ when I lie down,
Christ when I sit down,
Christ when I arise,
Christ in the heart of every man who thinks of me,
Christ in the mouth of everyone who speaks of me,
Christ in every eye that sees me,
Christ in every ear that hears me." [2]

Love is in us and with us. Love surrounds us.

Like you, I have already weathered many storms. But I am not overcome. I am honest about the hard things, but truly, I live with *great* joy. My heart is at rest. Peace goes beyond my understanding and doesn't even make sense in light of the circumstances. There are some losses I hope I will never experience, *but even if I do,* I know I will be okay.

I walk boldly and with confidence even while holding on for dear life, knowing that whatever comes, Love is with me. Love is bigger. And this fills me with hope.

Chapter 4

No One. No Thing.

"You have made us for yourself and our hearts are restless until they find their rest in thee."

ST. AUGUSTINE

We like to believe that for every craving, there is a satisfying agent. For every want, there is fulfillment. For every ache, there is a remedy. For every heart longing, a requiting love.

When I crave something sweet, a Reese Peanut Butter Cup is exactly the cure. And if I can't have that, I melt peanut butter and chocolate chips together in the microwave. When my brain is fried, I need Netflix. When I have the kind of stress that makes my heart pound, I want a glass (bottle) of red wine. When I have bone-deep exhaustion, I need a nap. When I long for connection, I want coffee-time with friends. When I need a creative re-boot, I orchestrate a time of solitude. When my thoughts are jumbled, I need journal time. When my feelings can't escape my body, I sit at the piano and allow music to say what words cannot. When I have pent up frustration, I head out for a power walk. When my brain is relentlessly busy, I am quieted with list-making and meditation.

I wanted academic success to fulfill me, and though I am proud of what I've achieved and have grown in learning, it has not quenched the desire for more. I believed a life partner would fulfill a deep soul-longing, but even our 'person' cannot fully satisfy the ache to be truly known. Though I know better, I really felt like renovating our home would feel good. And it did, in a way. I value esthetics and I love our physical space, but that's as deep as it goes.

We have ways to meet our needs. Or, at least, to quiet them. To numb them. Temporarily. Momentarily. Detrimentally?

The distasteful news is that no one and no thing will permanently satisfy your deepest need. There is no once-and-for-all miracle.

Not alone time. Not friend time. Not coffee. Not a dog. Not a different job. Not a new hair color. Not a new sofa. Not having a baby. Not meeting the right person. Not bigger biceps. Not a different church. Not your children. Not your husband. Not chocolate. Not wine. Not Netflix. Not size 6 pants. Not a hot bath. Not Advil. Not a different partner. Not more success. Not a new pet. Not food. Not *no* more food.

No one. No thing.

C.S. Lewis says that *"we live with a God-shaped hole in our hearts."*[1]

Created things and constructs are meant to be enjoyed, meant to add to the human experience. But we are not only physical beings. So physical things do not quench the eternal thirst. They cannot satiate the divine hunger. They do not fill the hole.

We become quickly dissatisfied. We leak. We need constant infilling.

The only satisfying agent for every soul hunger, every unquenchable thirst, and every longing is divine. For some of us, that means Jesus. For some of us, that means the Great Spirit. Or the Universe. Or another name for God. Regardless of the name you use, humans straddle two worlds. With one foot in our concrete, physical experience, and the other firmly floating in the realm of spirit, we live in limbo. We see as through a glass darkly. We are in the *now* and the *not yet*. The fulfilled and the unfulfilled. Though we experience moments of connection when heaven touches earth, we cannot arrive and set up camp at *fullness*. Regrettably.

Perhaps the answer is to simply notice and embrace the empty feeling when it arises. To live with great love and empathy for ourselves and for others, awake to the ache that is intrinsic to all of humanity. Instead of attempting to outrun the void, or stuff it to full with lesser things, why not cherish and protect this space that is intended only for divine connection?

In the interim, I don't believe we are meant to merely endure this world. We don't have to scrape by, longing only for "heaven." I am fully aware that the combination of peanut butter and chocolate isn't the fullness of heaven, but for me, it's a taste of heaven. I know that Netflix cannot compare with true inner peace, but I certainly embrace it as a gift in this moment. My kids are imperfect humans who are mostly wonderful and are sometimes jerks, but we love whole-heartedly, even if imperfectly. For me, they are a taste of the fullness.

We are meant to live wholly in the now and the not yet. We are made to enjoy God and enjoy others. The place of longing is by design.

Though I, like you, live with the God-shaped hole, I am simultaneously filled with great joy and peace along the journey. We may not live in the perpetual fullness, but we can embrace every small, joy-inducing measure with gratitude along the way. And this, my friends, is divinely satisfying.

Chapter 5

The Whole Damn House

---

*"We can not selectively numb emotions. When we numb the
painful emotions, we also numb the positive emotions."*
BRENÉ BROWN

You are a hugely gorgeous house. You have many rooms. You were
made this way. So, why are you camping out in one room?

God talks to me. Very Joan of Arc, I know. But I'm not special in
this. The divine speaks to you and to *all* of us if we're paying attention.

As parents, we communicate with our children in unique ways,
according to who they are and individualized by our relationship with
them. In the same way, we are spoken to in ways that are specific to us
and according to the unique friendship with us. The more we listen
and learn how God speaks to us, the easier it is to recognize the voice.
When my mom calls me on the phone, she doesn't have to say, "Hi
Ellen, it's Mom!" I talk with her *all the time*, so I know her voice. It's
the same with God.

I am a *words* person. I require a lot of words to explain my thoughts
and feelings, and when others share their words with me, it helps me
to feel loved. I might know in my heart that you love and appreciate

me, but when you *tell* me with your words, spoken or written, I *really* get it. Interestingly, I rarely hear words from God. Epiphany often occurs for me in the form of an image or picture in my mind; something visual that unfolds into analogy or allegory. Occasionally, there are accompanying words.

An image that I saw in my mind, many years ago now, was of a large, older house—an expansive and stately home with high ceilings and spacious, well-appointed rooms. It was so beautiful, and I was eager to explore. As I wandered through, it seemed that many of the rooms had been closed up, like a summer home prepared for a vacant winter season. Room after room, shutters were closed on windows, and dark drapes were drawn. Furniture was hidden under dust clothes. Discarded, broken items cluttered surfaces. Lights were extinguished and there was an absence of heat. Cold and dark. Uninhabited.

Eventually, I found one room which was lived in. In the whole of this glorious house, one small space had light, and heat, and life. The house, as it turns out, was me. And the accompanying words said, "Live in *all* the rooms of your house."

Many times, though the intention *is* for us to live in a spacious house with many rooms, we end up shutting things behind closed doors. Perhaps we want to escape painful experiences or memories. Shut the door. Maybe we feel ashamed when we remember something we've done or that was done to us. Shut the door. A relational breakdown that is never resolved. Shut the door. Refusal to forgive and bid bitterness good-bye. Shut the door. Hopes deferred and dreams in decay. Shut the door.

Before we know it, we find ourselves in a small space, existing in one meager room though the whole house is ours to inhabit.

It will require massive amounts of courage, but we need to open the doors. We need to walk into the rooms we've closed up and turn on the lights. Throw open the heavy drapes to illuminate what we've tried to hide, or forget, or ignore. We cannot live whole-heartedly when we're afraid of being found out, when we're hiding things, or when we're unwilling to deal with the hard stuff. Full freedom comes when we turn on the lights and see the monsters for what they are: not real, not powerful.

To paraphrase the brilliant thoughts of Brené Brown, *if you numb the hard stuff, you numb the good stuff.* Wouldn't it be lovely if we could carefully select the feelings we will feel? Throw open certain doors and windows but keep others locked up tight? But we can't have it both ways. When we attempt to limit pain, fear, and embarrassment, we unwittingly shut down joy, peace and gratitude.

Before you apply the "Jaws of Life" to the chained and dead-bolted doors on the rooms in your house, remember that Love is kind and compassionate. Ask for guidance with your process. Sometimes memories will gently resurface, or our attention will be drawn to something specific, and we can simply consent to the journey. At other times, we might need to be more intentional about going after things, especially those we know still have a hold on us. We can ask God to walk us through it; we can invite and receive healing. Nobody loves dealing with their pain, but there is no way through it but through it. And it's so worth it. As you've no doubt heard, courage isn't an absence of fear; it is feeling the fear and doing it anyway.

At the risk of sounding prescriptive, there are many things we can do to reclaim our houses.

Schedule time. We *have* to have time for process. We're often so busy and preoccupied with life that we rarely have quiet. Spend time reflecting. Write in your journal. Ask God to talk to you. It's in stillness that locked rooms will be drawn into our awareness.

Feel your feelings. If you have discomfort or pain about something, listen to it. Feel it. We need to get comfortable sitting with our pain. Open one of your closed doors and walk into the room. Sit there for a while. Cry. Groan. Be *angry*. Stay, even when you want to run out screaming. The Comforter, who I believe is God's Spirit, will meet you there.

Vulnerable admission: Sometimes I get really loud when I'm in my car by myself. I yell, I pray out loud, and sometimes I even groan … because, friends, though I love words, words cannot always express what needs to be said.

Ask for support, whether in the form of presence or prayer. That *thing* that is *so* hard or loud in your head can be rendered mute when we share it. Whether it's from trusted friends or family or your community, ask for what you need.

Forgive. We have to forgive—forgive others, forgive ourselves. Forgiving somebody is *not* a way of saying "what you did is okay." It's saying, "I'm unhooking myself from this heavy thing; it will no longer weigh me down or have a hold on me." And it's not a friendly suggestion; if we want to live fully, it's imperative.

Therapy is an invaluable resource. Talking to a professional counselor is my absolute favorite. Honestly, what could be better than someone who is being paid to listen to you? And they can't tell anyone else anything you say. And they ask you really good questions. There are no inane reasons for counseling. We all know that there are worse things in the world than what we are experiencing, but your experience is *your* experience. You're allowed to wrestle with it.

Honest moment: a few years ago, I spent time talking with a counselor about many things, but one of which was that my excessively urinating dog was bringing out a rage in me, the likes of which I have never experienced. True story. See, no dumb reasons.

As daunting as it may seem to open long-closed doors, the beauty is, when it's done, it's done. You don't have to be afraid that in entering a room, you'll never come out. Sure, we may go through a deeper level of healing on a same or similar issue at another time, but the more we face our hard stuff and experience the mental, spiritual, and emotional relief that comes, the more we understand it's worth it.

You are a hugely gorgeous house. You have many rooms. You were made this way. No more living like a hermit in one small space because your whole house is filled with garbage. Fling wide the doors. Clean it out. Let in the light. Live in your whole damn house.

Chapter 6

Less Like Scars, More Like Character

"Out of suffering have emerged the strongest souls; the most massive characters are seared with scars."

KHALIL GIBRAN

Not long ago, I read an article about maps that astounded me. Cartographers reveal that it is immensely difficult to distinguish between mountains and valleys on a topographical map. Something akin to an optical illusion occurs when we view them from an aerial perspective, from too far away. It takes getting closer to a mountain to know it's a mountain. It requires proximity to a canyon or valley to identify it as such.

The same can be true in our lives. So many times, from an aerial view, I have faultily categorized experiences as "bad" or "good" only to realize on closer inspection that the hard thing was *actually* a good thing, rich with meaning. And sometimes, the thing I'd deemed good *wasn't.*

In my home, short-sleeved shirts and long-sleeved shirts do not share the same pile. Random kitchen paraphernalia, like cork screws and pate knives, go in the second drawer down. Do not put the dessert forks with the dinner forks. They each have their own space.

I want life to be like this, too. I want everything that happens to fit neatly into its assigned drawer or cupboard or shelf. But, as we know, this doesn't happen.

I've thought about this a lot this year. It has come up in my conversations. It resurfaces in my journal. It gets referenced in my writing. And I feel that I have *finally* grasped how simplistic and errant this *good/bad* analysis has been. While it works for us occasionally, it fails us regularly. There is *not* always a place for everything, and everything *isn't* always in its place. I'm learning that most experiences in life can be assigned to either column, depending on how we look at them... how we frame and re-frame. And weirdly, many things can find their home in both columns, concurrently.

Our bodies are marked with memory and story. We are physical records, living artifacts. Some of the marks have pleasant memories attached. Some have painful memories attached. Many fall into the *"both"* category; things that hurt so much at the time, but that somehow became lovely. Our scars tell stories.

I have a shiny, circular scar on the inside of my ankle that has been with me for more than thirty years. It reminds me of the summer I was first allowed to venture out on my own to the busy, tourist-filled streets of Cavendish, Prince Edward Island. I would leave my home, high on independence, and scooter alone toward the Tourist Mart where I would buy a root beer flavored popsicle or maybe a Fun Dip. For a relatively flat province, there were many long hills that challenged my ten-year-old muscles. As I pushed my scooter along with my right leg, my bare ankle would often graze the brake; so regularly, in fact, that it didn't heal all summer long. And I still have the mark. It was worth it.

There are marks on my body that speak of embracing my individuality and coming into my own. Some of the choices made can still be seen, and some are ghosts. You can see the faded tattoo that remains from a visit to a random basement (I don't recommend this), but you can't see that I once had a buzz-cut (I, also, don't recommend this). While my nose still bears the piercing that my Doc Marten-wearing self sought out in Toronto a hundred million years ago, I have other empty holes on my body; left-over piercings no longer filled with jewelry. But I remember the rush of every single one. It was worth it.

My belly looks like a treasure map with X-shaped scars literally marking the spots. These faded scars can still make me weep this many years later when I remember the life that grew in the wrong place and the rupture that necessitated emergency surgery — a surgery that saved my life but also removed a tiny life from my body. I remember my first baby, and I am filled with gratitude that my life was spared. Though it hurt so much, I grew in trust and character. It was worth it.

I have a scar on my knee that still turns pink after a hot bath more than ten years later. I'd been boating with *min venner* (my friends) in the fjords of Norway and we pulled up to the rocks to barbecue steaks on an *engangsgrill* (a totally non-eco friendly one-use grill). Afterwards, we launched ourselves into the freezing cold water for a swim. It was so shockingly cold that I scrambled my way up a rocky ledge to escape imminent hypothermia. Frozen, I didn't feel my knee being shredded on the razor rocks. It hurt like crazy later, and it took forever to heal, but the scar still fills me with warm, sun-burned memories of being in one of my favorite places in the whole world. It was worth it.

When my children were younger, they remarked regularly whenever they saw the stretch-marked skin of my abdomen, *"Mama, why does your belly look funny?"* I always answered, *"Because you grew there. And you were so worth it."*

And now, as I've pushed further into my forties, I notice other marks on my body. I see evidence on my skin of time spent outdoors. And my eyes bear witness to many years of smiling. And it's been worth it.

But the external marks are not the only ones we bear. I have soul scars that can still be painful when pressed just so. Things that maybe didn't heal quite right and left ugly scars, something I'd rather not have as a part of me. But even *these* scars carry stories. If we accept the invitation, *even these* can produce character in us.

The painful ache of loss was because I loved him deeply, and it couldn't work, but I don't regret it. It was worth it. The sting of humiliation was because I attempted something brave and failed. But I'm still glad I did it. It was worth it. The sickening shame of self-awareness, realizing I acted selfishly and immaturely, taught me to own my weakness and seek help. These were all hard lessons that were worth it.

We get to decide how we read situations, how we view our scars. Are they evidence of damage done or evidence of healing that occurred? Are they painful reminders of regret or are they experiences that have added valuable patina, contributing to our character?

We hold physical, spiritual, and emotional records *in us* and *on us*. It's inevitable. So, while some may see stretch marks, creases, aging skin, and soul scars, I'm choosing to see the story of where I've been so far. I'm looking carefully at the *perceived good* and the *perceived bad*. I'm treasuring *all* of it, recognizing that, sometimes, the parts I thought were valleys were actually mountains. All of these stories have contributed to who I am and to who I'm becoming.

As time passes, the marks are looking less like scars and more like character.

Chapter 7

Not Dead

"Hold fast to dreams, for if dreams die, life is a broken-winged bird that cannot fly. Hold fast to dreams, for if dreams go, life is a barren field, frozen with snow."
LANGSTON HUGHES

The story of Lazarus is a shot of adrenaline into a failing heart. You see, the story of Lazarus isn't just about Jesus raising a physical body from the dead. It's a story about speaking life to things that are dead. Like really dead. Too far gone dead. Stinking dead. Impossible dead. Grieved and over dead.

There are times when I can't discern whether a piece of writing should remain in the vault of my private journal or be vulnerably shared with the world. This is one of those times. Though this exhortation was certainly intended for me, I feel a sneaking suspicion it might be for you as well. So, I'm opening up my journal.

Here's a brief synopsis of the story of Lazarus, in case you haven't heard it:

He was sick, like, *really* sick. His sisters, Mary and Martha, contacted Jesus to come quickly (they knew he could heal the sick). Jesus got the news and took his time (nice one, Jesus). Lazarus died (umm, what?!). His body was prepared for burial and placed in a tomb. Jesus finally showed up days later. The sisters were upset (and, maybe, *really freaking mad?*) that he hadn't come in time to heal Lazarus. When Jesus arrived, they had already said a final good-bye to their brother. They were already grieving. They had already lost all hope for his healing. It was over. Or so they thought.

They didn't fully understand that Jesus isn't only a healer. He's a resurrector.

What have you declared dead, wrapped in burial clothes, and placed in a grave? Perhaps it's a dream that wasn't fulfilled like you'd thought, and so, you've set it adrift. Maybe you've been praying for years for rescue from addiction or chronic illness—and it seems so many years have been wasted. Did you receive a word of promise, but now you're questioning, *"Did God really say ... ?"* It may be that there is a relationship in your life, like a marriage, that has been wasting away—it has been on death's doorstep for so long, or has maybe ended, even though the piece of paper still says otherwise.

I feel strongly that some of us may need to roll back the stone and have a look inside our tombs. What has died for you? Not because you *wished it* dead, and not because it was left untended or neglected, but because the circumstances didn't change, the timeline ran out, the miracle didn't come.

It's terrifying to enter those dark places of disappointment, to willingly re-visit hopes and dreams that have faded into non-existence, or to re-open those deaths already grieved.

When I summon my courage, roll back the stone, and enter my own tomb, I observe several hopes, dreams, and plans wrapped in burial clothes. Some of the plans died a natural death. Some of the hopes and dreams that died *needed* to die. They had their origin in my own ideas and ambitions.

In my younger years, I dreamed of auditioning for Broadway musicals. I was going to arrive at a cattle call and have the casting producers realize they'd found their new lead girl … Les Mis's Eponine, or Rent's Mimi. I've performed in a number of local musical theater productions in the past, but the unrealistic Broadway dream has drifted on by. And it's really okay. I have chosen a life here with my family (and let's be honest, I wasn't going to make it past the first cut, anyway—also problematic is that I am not the ideal ethnicity intended for any of the roles I desired).

These dreams fade or alter with relative ease. We grow older, we mature, we determine who we really are. Though we might experience regret or loss, wishing things had played out differently, we can also be pragmatic in our analysis, able to understand (and possibly even appreciate) why the particular thing *didn't* happen. They are light things, easily blown around, and carried away like dry leaves.

But, my friends, there are other promises and dreams that *don't* die easily. They are weighty, deeply buried, substantial things. You know the ones I mean. The ones that we struggle to release. That we cannot seem to get over. That maybe we *shouldn't* get over. But because they didn't get fulfilled according to *our* timeline—because Jesus didn't show up when we thought he would have done, or should have done—we declare it *over*. We didn't want to let it go, but by all human accounts, it was very obviously dead. So we buried it.

These are the longings, the plans, and the promises that were placed in our DNA when our bodies and persons were formed. *And even though we've declared some of these things dead, Love views it differently.* If we can be brave enough to re-enter the tomb, Love will highlight the ones that are active and living, even though our natural eyes may not perceive it.

As in the story of Lazarus, Jesus isn't restricted by our timelines, or bound by our natural laws. Jesus isn't inhibited by dead things. He doesn't look at your dream or your situation and say, *"Argh! I should have got here sooner. Damn it … sorry about that!"*

The writer of Romans talks about the "God who gives life to the dead and calls things that are not as though they were."[1] I love this. It doesn't become *harder* for God to restore, redeem, and renew once something has died.

When there is no response, according to *our* preferred timeline, it's not a lack of care for us, nor that there is no intention of keeping the promise. It's because there is a larger story. A story authored by Love.

When Jesus arrived at the home of Mary and Martha, four days after Lazarus had died, the sisters were understandably upset. Jesus says to them, *"I am the resurrection and the life. The one who believes in me will live, even though they die; and whoever lives by believing in me will never die. Do you believe this?"*[2]

We are asked the same question: "Do you believe this?" Yes. I believe it. I believe that you will breathe life into things that I have laid to rest, dreams that have fallen asleep in the waiting. I believe you will call things that are not as though they are. I believe. Help my unbelief.

The miracle is not late. Love has not let us down. If it has been spoken, it will be fulfilled. Love does not disappoint. The resurrection comes at exactly the right time. Oh, how I need to remember this.

Chapter 8

Tapestry

"The dark and the light, they exist side by side. Sometimes overlapping, one explaining the other. The darkened path is as illuminated as the lightened ... "

RAVEN DAVIES

Have you ever looked closely at a woven tapestry? It requires many, many colors and varieties of thread to achieve an overall image. Weavers understand that you cannot choose only your favorite tones or your one preferred medium and then begin. Though you may intend for a certain color to be prominent, it takes others—light and dark—to truly magnify and highlight the overall pattern. While you may love the silk, gold, and silver warp threads, without the necessary weft threads, often made from regular old cotton or linen, the image cannot be created.

I am a magpie. I love to surround myself with bright, shiny things. Superficially, if I could, I would have all of the beautiful colors and experiences and feelings in my nest, and *none* of the hard things. However, on a more pragmatic level, I know this never works.

Any time attempts have been made to that end, the result is a one-dimensional, Polly-Anna, bubblegum, Pleasantville-like experience.

It's hollow and false. It lacks the depth and nuance and richness that comes from hard-won battles, honesty, and walking it out, no matter what.

There are parts of my life and my story that hold beauty and provide joy in the remembering. Some of my favorite, shiny filaments have been synergy in partnership, intimate friendships, my passionate children, feeling meaningful in my job, the ability to create music, and the spiritual heritage extending down both sides of my family tree.

But some fibers in my history feel like they've woven an indelible stain or a darkness that I'd rather not revisit. The dark strands are those shadow times when I knew I'd veered from the path intended for me but couldn't seem to climb back up from the ditch. The dark strands are the things I never wanted in my story: anxiety, disappointment, heart break, divorce.

And then, there are those seasons of 'non.' As someone who feels deeply and who is quite "Anne of Green Gables" in terms of my highs and lows, this place of mundane, dreary, middle ground is *not* my favorite. These are the times that are neither good nor bad, they just are. The waiting, treading water seasons that lack enough discomfort to drive us into God but that don't contain enough joy to remind us we are living.

But all of these threads—the light, the dark, the neutral; the common, the rare, the breathtaking—together, they contribute to the total design.

With maturity and a more seasoned perspective on life, I've learned to live engaged in the moment. I am not, by nature, a person who remains easily in the present. I tend to reflect on the past, wallowing in nostalgia and regret, *or* I strain toward the future, dreaming of and planning for what will be. While I agree that great contentedness comes from staying awake in our everyday lives, I also believe there *can* be value in looking behind, in turning around to gaze over what has been. Where I've come from. Not for the purpose of entertaining regret or shame, but in a way that allows me to learn from and appreciate the overall pattern.

A number of years ago, I listened to a wonderful Indigenous speaker, Terry LeBlanc, talk about walking backwards into the future.[1] This notion speaks to the value that can be gained in remembering and understanding our pasts. It's about allowing where we've been to inform where we are going. It resonated greatly with me.

For some of us, the idea of looking back over our lives produces dread or fear. We don't *want* to remember what was, whether the good or the bad. Perhaps in remembering the 'good old days,' we wonder if we've passed our prime; are our pinnacle days behind us? Looking back, thus, leaves us sad and longing for what was. Or maybe, what was behind was hard. Evil, even. The thought of reliving any part of it, even in the thinking of it, causes a vehement reaction to run, to turn away, to slam the door. Or perhaps we feel shame when we look behind, because we turned subtly or severely from what we knew was right. As a result, we experience regret and guilt when we remember things done and not done.

But here is what I know. When we take a deep breath, summon our courage, and choose to turn around, what we see will take our breath away.

When I reflect on my life, thus far, I feel both a healthy pride and some small amounts of disdain for my bone-headedness (we're making that a word). I live as a person forgiven, free of shame and regret, but I'm also self-aware and cognizant of my own flaws and errors. I've had strong faith ... and sometimes, I've chosen another path because I thought I knew better. I've worked to serve others and to bring healing ... and conversely, I've hurt others and myself. I have chosen over and over to remain aware of Love's closeness in the midst of difficult times … and also, I've done anything I could to escape pressure and to numb my pain.

When I gaze behind me, I *do* see the good, but I also see the deviations and mis-steps. I see the dark threads. If it were possible, I know I'd be tempted to root out those dark threads from my story. Wouldn't you? But were we to do that, the complexities and patterns that have been created wouldn't be what they are. You wouldn't be who you are. I wouldn't be who I am.

If God is a creator, and if God is unchanging, which most days I believe to be true, then God is *forever creating*. It's in a creator's nature to continue to create, and recreate, and redeem, and restore, and utilize every. single. part.

While we tend to see events, experiences, and feelings in isolation, categorizing them as "good" and "bad," (especially when we're in the middle of a season and don't have a bird's eye perspective), a creator sees it all as valid and useful material. When we offer our raw material, a creator can make use of everything. God uses all the material of our lives to weave the most intricate and beautiful tapestry. The individual strands of disappointment and pain and joy and surrender get woven together in such a way that the overall image is beauty.

I don't believe that God causes pain or inflicts illness. I think it's simply part of the human experience—the result of living in an imperfect world with imperfect people. But I certainly *do* believe that Love can weave together something beautiful with all the fibers of our lives. And it's not done yet.

Take a big breath. Tell your regrets, and your shame, and your fear to be quiet. And then, turn around. Have a look at the tapestry flowing out behind you; the masterpiece extending from the loom of your life. It's lovely and complex, light and dark. And altogether, it's beautiful.

Elemental

(Earth, Wind, Fire, Water)

Chapter 9

Shake Up to Wake Up

"Now, everytime I witness a strong person, I want to know: What dark did you conquer in your story? Mountains do not rise without earthquakes."

KATHERINE MACKENETT

An earthquake can be a devastating force. My early years were lived in southern California where benign quakes were a regular occurrence and it was no big deal to see water sloshing in the neighbor's pool. But I have also seen with my own eyes the aftermath of a massive quake in Haiti that left the country in ruins. Earthquakes can ravage in minutes what has taken years or decades to build.

Recently, while meditating, I saw a picture in my *mind's eye* of a tall skyscraper rocking back and forth. It was almost as if it had become rubberized and was swaying, Gumby-like, side to side. It was evident an earthquake was occurring. The ground heaved, and the building trembled and shook. But it didn't fall. It had been built for this.

There are a number of ways to earthquake-proof buildings. One way to make a simple structure more resistant is to tie the walls, floor, roof, and foundations into a rigid box that holds together. Another engineering masterpiece is to incorporate a massive water tank at a high elevation within a building to absorb the vibrations of seismic activity. Something like a giant pendulum has also been suspended into the center of skyscrapers with the goal of counterbalancing the lateral movements of the earthquake. Whatever the design, these are not technologies typically included in regular construction. They are intentional, preventative measures.

Preparation and proper engineering can be the difference between *still-standing* and rubble. The same is true for humans.

Like buildings that are designed to handle the vertical load of a roof and walls, we can typically support the vertical load of regular life bearing down on us: schedules, jobs, expectations, budgets. But earthquakes present a lateral or sideways force to structures that is more complicated to account for. These unexpected, sideways motions in our lives might look like infidelity, job loss, or a cancer diagnosis. Bracing against these quakes requires a more intentional design.

I am determined to withstand life's quakes ... and not *only* to withstand. I want to *stick it* to those unexpected lateral forces, repurposing them into something that serves instead of destroys.

Regretfully, I don't believe we're born ready. Yes, some humans have a naturally higher level of resiliency, but more often, it's a case of being retro-fitted, which is always uncomfortable, messy work. But necessary work.

There have been seasons in my life that I didn't understand at the time. In retrospect, I can see that what felt destructive was an intentional, preventive measure. I was being quake-proofed.

Remember when you felt gutted, like your fragile insides were being removed but possibly being replaced with something much stronger? It was for this. Remember when it felt like your foundations were crumbling, jack-hammered, and bull-dozed? It was for this. Remember when you got dug down so deeply that you wondered if you'd ever see the light of day again? It was for this. Remember when you were deconstructed to the point that you no longer even recognized yourself or your faith? It was for this.

When we've been made strong by engineer-God, we can withstand and even prevail. The quakes that threaten to take us down might make us sway and crumble a little. We might shudder and tremble, but baby, we won't fall.

Divine presence in us literally acts as the counterbalancing force against life-quakes. When the lateral pressures come and we are swayed, God-in-us stabilizes us. Where once we would have been devastated, now, we stand firm.

Permission to speak freely? Metaphorically, of course.

Sometimes a little earthquake *isn't* the worst thing in the world. What might be intended for evil can be used for good. If we want to be our truest and best selves—if we want to discover *essence*—we *need* some things to fall away. And a quake is the very thing to accomplish it.

It is frighteningly easy to float along, ignorant and self-absorbed, deaf and blind to our own ideas, beliefs and passions.

We don't even know what we think about things.

We grip batons of opinion handed to us like they're our own.

We wear mantles that do not align with who we were created to be.

We define ourselves by uninvited labels that were slapped onto us by others.

We tout beliefs that actually hold very little resemblance to divine goodness.

We enable relationships that are hazardous to our health.

We gird with extra layers of protective padding that end up isolating us.

Sometimes we *need* a little shake up to wake up.

In my early thirties, the ground shook and it all fell down. While my building was technically still upright, I experienced a deconstruction that altered every aspect of life as I had known it, no part left untouched. My beliefs swayed, my family structure altered, my understanding of my place in the world trembled, and my sense of safety, belonging, and meaning shook. The facade crumbled and my building was beyond recognition.

During this time, I experienced something like a vision or a thought-process or a movie in my mind; you can choose whatever language you're comfortable assigning to such inexplicable experiences.

I saw myself crouched before something like a giant pile of broken concrete and rubble; a mountain made up of the debris of my life. I was on my hands and knees, hunched over and overwhelmed. I couldn't discern what was worth saving and what was lost, what was God-made and what was human-made, what was truth and what was lies. It was all mixed up together in that giant mountain before me—a mountain I knew was mine to sort through.

And then I became aware of a presence; someone was with me. To my right, I pictured Jesus on his knees beside me. Sobbing and gasping, I said, *"Jesus, I just can't ... oh my god, I just don't even know where to start!"* He looked at me, face full of understanding, then gave me a wink of solidarity that said, *"Right, let's do this."* He pushed up his Jesus-sleeves, pulled my burden across his own shoulders, and began the sorting. As he pulled out each bit of rubble, he'd look at it, and then look at me, *"This is garbage. Pitch it. This is truth. Put it in the keep pile. This isn't love. Get rid of it."* And so on.

The *vision* went on for quite a long while. I remember the absolute comfort and safety of his presence. I felt held. He was with me. And when the sorting was complete, I had a drastically smaller pile than when I began, one I could hold in my two hands. But it was truth.

My building looked more bare-bones and less ornate, but it was truly, authentically me.

This *epiphanal* experience (urban dictionary agrees with me that epiphanal should be a word) has remained with me throughout the years. The earthquake was worth it. I still hold these most important God-truths like precious treasures. There are a lot of ideas and patterns, habits and rules to which we blindly adhere that don't actually have their origin in God. They are cultural norms, mores, practices—not *all* bad, but not always that important. I'll take a small handful of treasures I know to be genuine over a giant mountain of rubble any day.

So, this quake you're experiencing right now? The truth is, it may leave you a little banged up. It might cause a few fractures in your structure. Your beautiful facade may crumble and you might not even recognize yourself. You're gonna feel it all. But God is within you. You will not fall.

Let's reframe the inevitable quakes of life for good instead of devastation. When we are fortified, earthquake experiences can, surprisingly, serve us well. They shake our foundations enough to wake us up and to remove the accumulation of non-essential crap we carry around with us. We don't have to be afraid of these quakes.

Love holds all things together. That includes you.

Chapter 10

Deadhead

---

*"The purpose of pruning is to improve the quality
of the roses, not to hurt the bush."*
FLORENCE LITTAUER

My life is an enormous metaphor. The more I've learned about myself, especially through the lens of the Enneagram[1], the better I have understood that not everyone ascribes meaning to elements of life in the same way that I do. There are occasions that I read into situations and find meaning where there isn't any, but there are others where the insight is immeasurably useful and helps me to understand important things. I truly believe that metaphor is one of the ways the divine speaks to me.

My morning routine has involved coffee, journaling, and prayer my entire adult life. In fact, my preferred perch in our living room is made plain by the indent on our sofa. I've tried to move around so as not to permanently imprint my bottom on that one cushion, but it just doesn't feel right.

Often, I begin with a self-assessment of how I am entering the day: *How did I sleep? How do I feel? What lies ahead today? What am I thankful for?* All of this can be thought or written. Next, I'll engage with a short reading or chapter to focus my thoughts. Then, I'll sit quietly with my eyes closed, listening for what God has to say. It is typically during this intentional quiet or meditation that I sense what Love is speaking. As I mentioned above, it is common for understanding to be communicated to me with images and metaphors.

On one such morning, my thoughts were drawn to the African violet sitting on my coffee table, right beside my crossed feet. It was massive. I had never done never anything special for it—and yes, I know that African Violets like to soak up water through their roots (holy, high maintenance!)—but I'd always just dumped it on top. Because I cannot be bothered. (Side note: I love plants and green things, but I've adopted a rather Darwinian stance toward the plants in my house. This is what you get. Deal or don't deal. Survival of the fittest, baby). In spite of the standardized treatment, this hardy violet was perpetually covered in beautiful, bright purple flowers.

However, that morning on closer observation, I realized that sections of the flowers were dead. They stood upright among the viable blooms, looking very much alive and purple, but they were dried out.

I was suddenly overcome with an intense compulsion to pick off the dead flowers—a crisis situation that felt bigger than dead flowers on a plant. Deadness in the form of bloom and leaf was draining energy from the parts that were alive! The initial early-morning task became a rampage throughout my entire house (yes, I can be a little intense). With a grocery-store bag in hand, I attended to every plant in my home, removing dry blooms and dead leaves. It took ages and made a mess, but in the end, I felt like I'd accomplished something tremendously healthy for my plants. And, strangely, also for myself.

Deadhead is a term that refers not only to the appreciators of Jerry Garcia (of whom I was one), but to the removal of faded or dead flowers from plants. It's generally done both to maintain a plant's appearance and to increase its overall health and performance.

Deadheading is tedious, but important work. Most flowers lose their allure as they fade, diminishing the overall appearance of a garden or individual plant. As flowers shed their petals and begin to form seed heads, energy is focused into the development of the seeds, rather than the flowers. Regular deadheading, however, re-directs the energy into the flowers, producing healthier plants and sustained blooming.

Deadheading can feel like a never-ending chore. It can also feel like your plant looks a little less full and alive once you've removed the deadness because sometimes, as was the case with my African violet, the *faux* blooms still *looked* alive. They were pretty and gave the illusion of a full, healthy plant. But they were dried and dead. Not alive. Sometimes it's hard to get rid of the blooms that *seem* alive.

Some things, in my humble opinion, *are* actually better *faux*. I regularly sport a "genuine pleather" (aka "vegan leather") jacket that is my absolute fave. My closet houses A LOT of faux fur, and there are giant faux-wolf throw pillows in my living room. Some things are better faux, but others are not. You are not good *faux*. Your life is not good *faux*.

Applying this measure of thought to my own life, I began asking questions. What looks like the real thing, but is not the real thing? What seems alive but is perhaps dried and dead? What is diverting energy away from the living parts? What do I need to deadhead?

On the simplest level, deadheading may need to happen in the form of purging excess from our homes, dealing with physical clutter, and donating our extras.

Maybe deadheading means simplifying our schedules. Determining what parts *need* to stay and then getting ruthless with the optional items. What *used* to be good but has now begun to deplete precious energy? What needs to go?

Is there a relationship that needs to go? This one is challenging, for we remember how beautiful these blooms once were. And if we squint, they can still *seem* alive; even though, in honesty, we know their season has passed.

What about those experiences in our personal histories that harass us over and over, diverting life—peace, joy, contentment, security, self-worth—away from the richness and health of our *now* life? We're usually aware of the things that continue to grip us like childhood hurts that never fully healed, the pain of rejection, broken relationships, the residual fear or poverty mentality from a season of lack, the inability to forgive.

For some of us, there may even be a deeply hidden fear that if we remove dead blooms, there will be nothing left. That *could* happen. At least for a period of time. I don't know about you, but I'd rather have a few vibrant blooms than many dried, dead blooms.

The thing about deadheading is that we can never check it off our list permanently (which I hate … I like doing jobs once). It's a practice that must be undertaken regularly if we want to be strong and healthy, blooming continually in season. If we haven't been in the habit of deadheading our lives, at first it may feel like a massive undertaking. But as it becomes part of our regular routine, a quick scan and an occasional pluck are all that are required.

Take some time to observe your life. Give attention to your soul. What is pretending to be alive, but is no longer alive? Ask God to show you what is no longer life-giving for you. Then do the work. Your vibrant, alive parts will reap the benefits. Your authentic self will thank you.

Chapter 11

Reclaiming My Garden

"Do not be dismayed by the brokenness of the world. All things break. And all things can be mended. Not with time, as they say, but with intention."

L. R. KNOST

In my corner of the world, flourishing gardens are a bold, lofty, and often unrealistic idea. Because deer. Seriously. Many, many deer.

I've essentially given up on the flower gardens that surround our home. There are approximately four varieties of plants that the deer won't eat, and so, that is what I grow. A whole garden filled with boxwoods, lavender, and geranium-based plants. But my vegetable garden is worth fighting for.

For more than a decade, I've planted a vegetable garden each spring. It is guarded by seven-foot high fences to keep out the deer. But deer are not the only pests. In order to deter rabbits and raccoons, the bottom half of the fences are overlaid with orange netting that extends into the ground. It looks terrible, and I'm sure my neighbors hate it, but it works. The garden contains raised beds with boards wide enough to perch on while I weed. Though I've attempted to thwart the pathway-weeds with landscape fabric, newspaper, mulch, and even gravel, the walkways refuse to remain level or tidy. *(I get it, pathways. I don't like to be contained either).* The wood components are showing their age with weathered posts and boards. The raised beds are no longer level because of frost heaves. In spite of the mess, it's lovely to me.

This messy garden has produced beans, peas, beets, carrots, cucumbers, potatoes, greens, parsnips, zucchini, tomatoes, pumpkins, herbs, and more. In addition to a primary harvest, we have also enjoyed by-products like pickled beets, salsa, relish, and zucchini muffins.

But it has given far more than healthy food for my family. It has provided years worth of memories with my children. It taught them that vegetables come from the earth, not from a grocery store. When they were little more than toddlers, I'd send them up to the garden with a bag to pick what they wanted for supper. It taught them to love food that they might otherwise have despised, simply because they had harvested it themselves.

My garden has been a place of solitude where I've been able to think my thoughts. It's been a place where I've escaped my own noisy head and connected with the earth. I can pull off *fancy*, but I'm a dirt girl. There is nothing quite like weeding and digging in soil to settle me.

Each spring, I have returned to my garden. I've pulled out weeds, replenished beds, bolstered fences, and nourished soil. Though a mammoth endeavour, it is immensely satisfying work.

Except … last spring, I didn't even walk to our back field to look at it.

Though outwardly you might not have known because I continued to smile, to work diligently, and to show up in my life, inside I was broken. For a number of significant reasons. Healing and restoration required most of my energy, and as a result, there were many elements of my life left unattended. Some parts were abandoned because I just could not. Others were fallow by choice. It was a time of necessary sabbatical. I carefully decided what I would do, and possibly more importantly, what I would no longer do—or, at least, set aside for a time.

Some things had to go, and as I engaged sabbatical, I realized my vegetable garden was one of them. It was too much work, and I had too little reserve. I simply walked away, assuming it was forever.

I didn't foresee that it would only be for a season. Retrospectively, I now understand that my garden needed to lie fallow. And so did I.

Some would define *fallow* as neglected and unproductive...vacant. In our culture, lack of productivity is considered failure or wasteful. But farmers know that soil needs to be given rest. When we offer fields a reprieve from planting, it allows the soil to heal. The nutrients replenish and fertility returns.

This spring, I was ready to take back my garden.

It was overgrown and ugly. The fence posts were leaning in to the point that I couldn't even walk down one side of the space. Frost had heaved the beds many inches above the ground. The soil was depleted, both from being washed away, and because it had been stolen for other uses. Some of the planter boxes had decayed and crumbled. My precious garden was in shambles.

I had to restore the fences and boxes and re-establish pathways between planters. I had to work the rotting, organic matter of the last year into the soil. I had to weed and decide what to plant.

And as I did the work, I became rapidly awake to the idea that the garden was a metaphor for *me*.

I restored fences.

For me, this meant re-evaluating my boundaries. Boundaries are not to keep people out but to indicate *what is okay for me and what is not*. It's not a means of controlling other people; it's a way of caring for and loving one's self.

Boundaries also allow us to redefine spaces. This is in, this is out. This lives inside my fences, and this stays on the outside. This is safe for me, and this is not. Establishing healthy boundaries gave me permission to allot value to what is important to me, without apology, like lots of alone time.

You can have the best boundaries in the whole world, with seven-foot fences, and all the chicken-wire, but if you leave the gate wide open, even by accident (like I did the other night), damage can occur quickly. I went out in the morning, realizing I'd forgotten to clasp the gate after watering the evening before, and found that the tops of my beets were all gone *(and I like to eat those!)*, as were many of my tomato plants.

If you know something or someone is going to come into your garden and trample your precious plants, you're allowed to forbid it/them entrance. It's not mean. It's not paranoid. It's healthy boundaries. Make sure fences are firm and your gate is closed when needed. You get to decide who and what has access.

I decided what to plant.

It's my garden and I get to choose what grows there. I'm owning my own beliefs, likes, and dislikes. Just because you love carrots, doesn't mean I have to plant carrots in my garden. Just because you don't like zucchini, doesn't mean I can't plant a whole bed of those delicious beasts. And guess what else? Maybe I used to like growing potatoes, but now I don't. I'm allowed to change my mind. No apologies.

Deciding what will grow in my garden means that I must then remember what I planted, so that I can easily identify intruders that have sprung up uninvited. Often, weeds mimic the plants they accompany. Sometimes they're even pretty. And they are certainly persistent! Stay diligent. Do the work. Because they will deplete the soil of moisture and nutrients. They will choke out the healthy plants.

They will sometimes grow up and cast shadow. We need to discern residents from squatters.

For me, this has looked like differentiating what I *actually* believe from ideas and thoughts passed on in childhood, or through my Evangelical church upbringing. What is true Truth, and what is human interpretation? What is actually important for my well-being, and what seeks only to control me?

I made the shit work for me.

Have you ever pondered the difference between poop and composted manure? Though essentially the same thing—digested-waste—one has been worked through, composted, and rendered useful. The other lays obscenely on the surface, stinking, and doing *no one* and *no thing* any good.

When hard things happen, we get to decide whether to be a victim, or make it valuable. We can't always control crappy situations *(ugh, terrible, unintentional pun)*, and we certainly can't eliminate challenging issues entirely. But we *can* control how we respond to the situations and make them work for our benefit. We can smell like excrement and become a landmine for shoes, *or* we can do the work, till it down in, and allow it to enrich our soil.

No sane person would ever say that manure smells good. You're allowed to turn up your nose, gag a little, and cringe. But then, put it to work. Even if it was meant for harm, we can use it to become rich soil for growing.

Let's reframe the hard things. Instead of looking at it through the whining lens of "Why is this happening? Why does everything happen to me?," see it all as manure. It's easy to be thankful for the beautiful things. But manure is a gift, too. It's just in disguise.

For a whole year, I was fallow. But no more. I have found tremendous joy in reclaiming my garden—in reclaiming *me*.

Do not worry if your garden is in disrepair or has been fallow for too long. That place that has been neglected, depleted, abused, overgrown, unused, and ignored can grow new and healthy things. But personal growth and wholeness don't happen by accident. Set your intention. Get to work.

I've often said that I gravitate toward people who have experienced pain—who have walked it out well. I prefer them. There is a quality to a person who has done the work. There is a presence to someone who has experienced hard things. It lends an authenticity and authority to their words. It gives you the sense that life can rattle their cage, and they'll still thrive. It makes them feel safe and rich. It's the kind of person I desire to be.

And so, this is the work. To repair our fences. To decide what is allowed to grow. To see manure as a gift. To reclaim our gardens.

Chapter 12

Refined

"And once the storm is over you won't remember how you made it through, how you managed to survive. You won't even be sure, in fact, whether the storm is really over. But one thing is certain. When you come out of the storm, you won't be the same person who walked in. That's what this storm's all about."

HARUKI MURAKAMI

The storm I dreaded ravaged me. And it rescued me.

Things have been onerous in a manner not necessarily visible, or even easily explicable. While the quotidian continued along its usual and expected trajectory with intermittent periods of joy and frustration, ecstasy and drear, I became acutely aware of a spreading dryness. Scanning our landscape, I observed that areas, once lush, had become parched. Parts of our terrain had turned extremely and dangerously dry.

And all the while, an elemental pressure was building. We desperately needed the rain, but I lived with dread of the storm. I listened nervously for rumbling thunder and observed the sky for signs of electricity. One spark in this wasteland could mean devastation.

The configurations and details of our dreaded storms are individual and extremely personal.

Maybe, for you, the gathering pressure is financial. You've lived teetering on the edge, barely keeping your balance. You've attempted to outrun the impending inevitable, but now, faced with reality, you cower under the battering rain of bankruptcy and loss.

Maybe you have attempted to evade a worrisome health issue. You've ignored it and explained it away for too long before finally acknowledging it aloud. It's all in your mind, you hope. It's nothing to worry about, you pray. The physicians observe and test … and you wait. The phone rings, the thunder rolls in the sky, and you feel in your gut that life is about to shift.

Maybe it's a relationship that's been frustrating and so painful, in spite of your many attempts toward restoration. You've read the books; you've prayed the prayers; you've visited the counselors; you've had the conversations. But the storm clouds continue to gather, and the sky threatens to open. Perhaps it's sustained relational tension or even infidelity, suspected or confirmed. You'd never have imagined it possible, but you now stand overlooking the precipice of divorce.

Maybe your dreaded storm is a dark night of the soul or a total loss or restructuring of faith. You always thought you knew the answers. You tried to live faithfully. But now, large questions brew and swirl. And you know you must turn to engage them.

The storms we dread have this in common: they build over time and we live in the heaviness of them—waiting, ignoring, enduring, dreading, avoiding, slogging. The air is thick, suffocating, paralyzing. We try—oh, how we try—to fix our gaze on the positive, denying that the parched ground is smouldering, hot and dry, ripe for devastating fire. We pray for rain, but we fear the implications of the storm that will deliver the very thing we need. A tiny spark, combined with tinder-dry conditions, is all that is required for a catastrophic wildfire.

As for me, I kept one eye on the sky, trying to stay ahead of what I perceived would be the worst, most horrific thing. When lightning struck and the landscape of my life was ravaged by fire, the storm simultaneously broke. And the rain poured.

The storm that ignited the fire almost immediately contained the fire.

The blinding flash and deafening crash of the storm finally breaking was dreadful, but in retrospect, I've come to believe that the drought conditions and the gathering storm were *actually* the harder part.

Though we dread it, the eruption of the storm—the actual crisis moment—can be the very thing to break the pressure.

Last week, I heard rumbling thunder in the distance, and my thoughts launched a scenario I attempted to capture with words. Though very simple, it felt revelatory to me.

"I see a dark, foreboding sky and feel the brooding, angst-filled, low grade pressure of an impending storm. Lightning strikes, and with an overtly aggressive crack of thunder, the sky splits and drops begin to fall—giant, pounding drops. Slowly at first, but then faster. The drops conjoin to become a vertical flood. Releasing the pressure. Releasing the heaviness. Releasing the cloud sorrow that's been held, though only barely, for too long. I dreaded this, but now I see that with the breaking comes relief. The water pours; initially tears and anguish unleashed, but then, fresh water ... washing, rinsing, cleansing, quenching."

The fire that was burning in my brain—the painful sparking of synapses with every thought, every flash of memory, every replay— has been doused with cool rain. The fire is extinguished and the swelling pressure is relieved.

The fire is out. Yes, it burned furiously for a moment, but it's out.

In the aftermath of the storm I so dreaded, the atmosphere has changed. The air temperature is fresh and breathable. The thickness is broken, and I move with ease through what was but a short time ago stifling, constricting, and suffocating.

I didn't want this fire. I didn't seek this storm. But I notice something in its aftermath. The burning has removed chaff. The burning has removed facades. The burning has removed excess. The burning has removed ignorant certainty.

The fire was painful—sickening, undesired, charring, diminishing—and though memories of heat remain in my scorched skin, the rain has cooled and soothed.

The debriding will take time as the charred remnants of emotion, security, and illusion are removed. It's a tedious process, excruciating and ugly, but necessary for healing. This temporary pain is for restoration and regeneration. Superficially, there will be scars, but underneath, health abounds.

Though I grieve the loss of what was—what existed before—I embrace my new reality. My altered landscape. The storm hit and we were ignited, but the rain came and saved me from irreparable devastation.

So now, I rise. Face marred with soot and ash. Broken skin in the process of healing. I hold in my hands the precious and essential elements that resisted the fire. I have been refined. Love remains.

Beauty from ashes. Joy from mourning.

Chapter 13

Crashing Waves

"Many of us spend our whole lives running from feeling with the mistaken belief that you cannot bear the pain. But you have already borne the pain. What you have not done is feel all you are beyond that pain."

KHALIL GIBRAN

When waves of grief, fear, discouragement, hopelessness, frustration, and physical pain crash over us, we don't have to be tumbled. We can plant our feet, steady our legs, hang on tight, and hold our ground.

Grief is frustrating. Its borders are fluid and changing, rendering it difficult to define. It's experienced in as many ways as there are people on the earth. Certainly, humans do seem to navigate specific stages of grief, such as denial, anger, and bargaining, as identified by Elizabeth Kubler Ross.[1] Yet, even in this, it's rarely in defined succession or order. It's more of an *overlapping—concentric circle—retracing of steps—all at once—not at all* kind of gong show.

The instigators of grief are many. Whether it's the loss of a person, a job, an ideal, a dream, or our health, loss in *any* form causes humans to experience feelings of disbelief, anger, hopelessness, and pain.

During my own seasons of grief, those who have healed me the most are God and people. And when I say *healing*, I don't necessarily mean miraculous rescue and the total removal of pain. Sadly, in the absence of unhealthy numbing, that kind of escape is not really a thing for humans. I refer more to the provision of solace for my soul, a safe place for my pain, and a supply of physical, spiritual, and emotional support.

We were never promised a by-pass around hard things. We live in this world, and we are not immune to the human experience. What Love *does* promise is that we will not be alone.

Though we may feel the impact of raging waters and blazing fires, we are not overcome. Even when a loved one is sick. Even when a relationship implodes. Even in bankruptcy. Even in the face of infertility. Even in loneliness. Even when dealing with addiction. Even in depression. Even in job loss. Even in betrayal. Even in the mundane struggle that is life. There is comfort and solace in the midst of all of these hard things—a peace that goes beyond our understanding and doesn't even make sense in light of what is happening or *not* happening.

As for people, what is needed the most, especially initially, are the ones who simply let you feel what you're feeling. They don't try to coax you from your darkness or tell you that everything will be okay or that "God's going to work everything together for your good." *I know that he is (*to be read through gritted teeth), but in this moment, I'm going to need you to shut your face with any and all trite bandaids and platitudes (No offense. Love you!). For me, the most healing comes through the people who are willing to crawl into my darkness and sit with me there. The ones who admit that they don't know what to say or how to help, but assure me they are with me; that I'm not alone and they're not going anywhere.

My mom was one of the people who entered the darkness with me during one of my most grief-filled times. The details are personal and not only mine to share, but I can tell you this. I've lost people close to me to death. I've missed them so terribly and felt the aching loss of knowing I'd never see them again, but *this* grief was different. With death, it's a heart wound that, with time, will heal. Eventually. But this was a wound that could never fully heal because it was constantly being re-opened.

All I could do (all I can do) was (is) keep it clean and freshly bandaged.

For the better part of a year, when I couldn't bear to be alone, I'd pack a bag and arrive on my mom's door step. First, she would wrap her arms around me. Then, she'd wrap me up in a blanket and seat me in a rocking chair in her kitchen. She would always pray for me and often, she'd mix me a drink. I would rock and weep. And I would rage and reel with the extreme disparity between life *before* and life *after*.

Though I've never been in a severe accident that has left me broken physically, I have certainly been in "accidents" that have left me every bit as broken, emotionally, and spiritually. A conversation with my sister during her own season of extreme loss initiated the way in which I now understand grief.

Grief is like a wave, or waves, that crash over us. I'm not referring to pleasant whitecaps, lapping at our toes in the sand. There is no sunshine, there are no beach towels, and there are no smiling faces in this vignette. I'm talking about the huge curl you may or may not see coming from a long way off; the wave that takes your breath away and makes you prickle with fear. The wave that leaves you wondering whether to try and stay afloat, or run for your life. But you cannot rise above it, and it cannot be outrun.

It's not a lack of faith or trust in God to feel the fear and cry out when such a wave threatens to tumble us. There's no pretending it's all okay or denying that you feel like you might drown. There is nothing to be done ... but stand.

There are seasons for advancing and being victorious and there are seasons for just standing (which, arguably, takes as much or more faith and courage). Trusting is all that is required. Like waves do, the grief will crash hard … and then it will recede. And you'll still be standing.

Though I am occasionally ambivalent about many parts of the Bible, the Psalms remain my favorite because I value authenticity. David is brutally honest about how things are and how he feels, but after the vent, he always lands on: but *this* is who *you* are, God. This is what *you* say about my situation. You are good. You do all things well. I trust you.

Instead of running from the waves trying to crash over you and living in constant fear that they will, turn and plant your feet. Now, brace your legs. Steady yourself and lean in. Let them crash! The waves will recede and you will still be standing.

Chapter 14

Burn It All Down

Journaling was encouraged during my youth but did not evolve into a personally substantive practice until I was on the doorstep of adulthood, living solo across the ocean, and learning to process some very adult experiences on my own. It has served a variety of purposes for me. Though I now practice meditation and mindfulness on a regular basis, I believe that journaling was the original means by which I slowed everything down in my high-velocity, monkey brain and focused on one-word-at-a-time. My thoughts were limited to the speed by which I could physically write them down. To this day, I still write in an *actual* journal with an *actual* old-fashioned pen or pencil. It's almost contemplative for me. It slows the expulsion of my many words to a slow trickle and allows me to see and understand what I'm thinking and feeling.

I am an ambivert, which means I live uncomfortably straddled between the realms of introvert and extrovert. I really need my feelings and my ideas to exist outside of my own brain in order to organize them and make sense of them, but I don't necessarily want to share these private things with other humans. Journaling provides the answer to this dilemma. Writing in a journal offers a safe, non-judgmental place to share all of my best and worst ideas, my feelings of torment and ecstasy, my semi-regular existential crises, my doubts, my questions, and my gratitude. And no one is the wiser to my crazy. Journaling allows me to extrovert in an introverted way.

As a deeply spiritual person, journaling is, for me, a vehicle for prayer and contemplation. Every morning when I wake, I sleepily make my way downstairs, I pour my freshly brewed coffee (set to grind and perk 20 minutes before my alarm sounds), and settle into my spot on the couch. I open my journal, I write the date, and then I wait. I listen for my own heart. I listen for God. I listen for truth. And I write it down. Sometimes the understanding that comes as I listen forms the basis for future essays, but often it's simply the method by which my soul is centered and readied for the day ahead. In order for me to give fully in my life, I must first be filled.

And finally, journaling serves as a chronology of events, feelings, and process. Everything I have walked through in my life, joyous and horrendous, finds its way into my journals. Every conversation, whether prophetic, encouraging, critical, or destructive, finds its way into my journals. Every furious, angry response is first vented into my journal and then translated into a more gracious and appropriate for-mat. Every confusing thought and shocking revelation is first vomited in my journal, and then hopefully, read and understood later.

"In my later teens and early twenties, I began chronicling my every joy-filled, angst-filled thought; a practice which has continued to this day. You can't even imagine how many filled journals are being stored in my closet at this very moment. Sometimes the thought that I might die unexpectedly, leaving behind my innermost thoughts for

all the world to see, keeps me awake at night and sleepily scheduling a giant bonfire for the very next day." (from another of my burned journals)

It's always been a grave fear that my journals might someday find their way into the public realm, should anything ever happen to me. In fact, we have a pact in my family, since many of us write our truth, that we will destroy one another's journals in the event of our sudden deaths. Morbid, but necessary.

I treasured my boxes of journals for more than half of my life, but last year, I realized that, although the writing contained stories of joy and gratitude, the pages were mostly filled with pain. Journaling is how I have processed every single moment in my life.

If anyone were to read these pages, they would perceive me to be a deeply troubled, angst-filled human—one whose life has been fraught with pain, disappointment, heartbreak, betrayal, and abandonment. There are just so many sad stories! And while these events and feelings are all true, they are not who I am.

Who I am is resilient and whole, filled with faith and hope, courage, and wisdom, and the riches that come only from pressure, and struggle, and time spent in the dark. The words on the pages denote gritty perseverance through very difficult things that allowed me to be whole and well. It's not a story about a broken person. It's the journey of a healed person. But I don't think everyone would get that. And I would hate for that to be the story told of me.

And so, I decided to burn it all down. And the more I thought about it, the more it felt like a sacred event that would mark something meaningful for me. I didn't want to lose the memories, epiphanies, and poetry held in these books, but I *did* want to destroy the words that were never meant to keep—the words that had already served their purpose by transforming pain to wholeness, ashes to beauty, brokenness to strength. All of the events chronicled on the pages of these journals had already been grieved. Suddenly, hanging onto them felt like surrounding myself in little shrines to heartache and urns containing dead things.

I carried the storage boxes outside to my yard. I lit a fire, and then began placing the journals, one at a time, on the pyre.

Twenty-five journals.

Ten thousand five hundred pages.

Two million, one hundred eighty-four thousand words.

All gone in a matter of hours.

I worried I would experience a great loss. I wondered if it would feel like a funeral for my life. I expected it would feel like a massive waste of so many words.

But what it felt like was a *zeroing* of the calendar.

The terms B.C. (before Christ) and A.D. (anno Domini—*the year of our Lord*), sometimes known as BCE and CE, are used to label or count the years in our Gregorian calendar. It's largely understood that 1 B.C. and 1 A.D. are where the calendar "zeros" with the birth of Jesus, though the year zero does not exist.

As a side note, if you *ever* wondered whether or not I might be a giant nerd, I wrote my undergrad thesis on "*Time as a Social Construct.*" There. Now you know for sure. Back to journaling.

The burning of my journals created an ending of *the before* and a beginning of *the after*. A clean slate of sorts. Though certainly, life is never without disruption, and there will continue to be all of the frustrations and difficulties that come with being a human, symbolically, I left some things behind. I lightened the load.

When I opened to the first page of my brand new journal, post-bonfire, I wrote:

"Since apparently I now burn my journals, it seems there is no sense in spending money on them. Writing hardly even seems to make sense, if only for the purpose of burning. And yet, how can I not? I guess it's time to reframe the purpose. Journaling is not my autobiography. It's not meant as my legacy. It's not the whole story. It's simply a practice by which I process and understand. And that is enough."

Chapter 15

Keeping It Real I

In honor of the fact that we are talking about being real to be known, and for a laugh, allow me to disclose some honest and quirky things about me—*flasher moments*, if you will. If you had sanitized and safe ideas about who I was before this moment, I'm about to correct the error of your ways. In my humanity, I hope I'm your cup of tea, but if I'm not … I'm reminding myself right now that it doesn't mean there's anything wrong with me. *Deep breath*

I have never been able to refer to myself as a writer. To label myself as such felt self-important or boastful, like a pretentious exaggeration of the definition. In my mind, it equated to referring to myself as an athlete, when, truthfully, my athletic endeavours include begrudgingly walking my dog and sporadic yoga. One would think that a university diploma of English Literature bearing my name would help me to identify as a writer, but no. I've always been more comfortable saying things like "I'm an avid journaler" or "I process with written words." But if a writer is, by nature of the definition, one who writes, then it does apply to me and, thus, qualifies me for the label. Over the last while, I've felt compelled, and even required, to acknowledge and accurately label myself as a writer. Saying it out loud continues to be an uncomfortable fit, but I am making an effort to wear it.

✳

During my university years, and off and on since, I've dabbled in prostitution. Vocal prostitution, that is. Yes, I did live in the Red Light district of Vesterbro in Copenhagen for a while, though that was about serving sandwiches and coffee, not sex. I'm a singer, so to earn a little extra money when I was a student, I used to sing radio jingles. I didn't mention it to many people, but when the commercials would play, I would die a little inside, feeling like such a jezebel. I've also done commercials, more for the fun of it than for the financial payout. Once, while sitting in a hot tub in Jamaica, another Canadian stranger said, "Hey, weren't you in a commercial for Dooly's Pool Hall?" (a billiards joint), at which point I slid under the water and drowned.

I make my own life hard all the time with preconceived notions and expectations. Though I try not to, I often have ideal visions in my mind about how something will unfold and then, when it doesn't line up, I feel frustrated and disappointed. To illustrate, every year, I set up an elaborate Advent plan for my family. Last year, it was going to involve daily reflective readings. I could picture us sitting by the tree, sipping hot chocolate, deeply moved by the spirit of the season. Nope. The readings were clearly waaaay too long for them to endure. There was a lot of sighing and lolling around, and it usually ended with me getting mad because they were *ruining* Christmas! Put that on Facebook, friends.

What's real, and maybe a little embarrassing, about you, friend?

Relational

(Tales From My Tribe)

Chapter 16

Vomit. Yes, Really.

"When you stop expecting people to be perfect, you
can like them for who they are."

DONALD MILLER

Even healthy people get sick. And sick people throw up. And not always when it's convenient or when we're ready for it. In fact, that's usually never the case. This is the part where you, dear reader, decide to continue on with an iron stomach or turn away because yes, I really am going to discuss vomit. Stick with me, if you can; there's something to be learned here.

As a mom of two, I've done my fair share of vomit catching … and sometimes, *not* catching. There have been those middle of the night episodes that require leaning your child over the edge of the bathtub for a 3 am hair wash. There have been those too late, desperate cries of "Mooommm!" from the back seat of the car and then, the dreaded sound (and necessary roadside clean up, usually involving dirty car napkins and wads of grass from the ditch). I missed an iconic Canadian moment at the opening of the Vancouver Winter Olympics when, just as Wayne Gretzky was about to light the Olympic torches,

I heard one of my children running around the house calling for me, using words, tears, and throw-up sounds to get my attention. First, in the upstairs hallway, then in the living room, and finally, at the top of the (carpeted) stairs to our family room. Sigh. Sorry, Wayne. I missed your big moment. I have caught puke in half-drunk cups of Starbucks coffee, balled-up-clothing-turned-catching-mitt, grocery bags still containing food items and, certainly, even in my hands.

A throw-up story that stands out among all the others happened just moments from my own driveway. My son had been complaining of feeling carsick, which he often did. So I placated him, which I often did. But in this instance, I wasn't taking him seriously enough. Clearly. Just moments from home, he erupted. I desperately reached around to pass him a half-eaten bag of Goldfish crackers which he held in his hands, proceeding to oscillate his face, aiming in every direction but the Goldfish receptacle.

My daughter was initially filled with great compassion for her big brother, who was in distress. Her initial sounds were of sympathy and kindness, cooing her comfort like a little mama: "It's okay, Co." and "We're almost home, bud." Until she caught wind of the smell.

As it wafted to her side of the vehicle, she began to gag and retch as well. Her dialog moved rapidly from compassion to disgust and demands for self-preservation. I'm laughing my head off even as I remember this, just as I did when both of my kids were throwing up in the back seat. I rolled down windows and comforted them through snorts of laughter. Because that is how these situations affect me.

This particular incident impacted me on a level more visceral than vomit. In the aftermath, as I attempted to clean my car (which consequently, though clean, smelled foul on warm days for a very long time), I contemplated how, in theory, we want to be the kind of people who can come alongside others. We want to be able to handle the hard stuff. We like the idea of being the support network for people during their dark nights. But theory is different than practice, and, like the *compassion turned disgust* in the car, we can become easily repulsed when sick people actually get sick. Because sick people do throw up. And it's messy. And it smells bad. And you might get caught in the crossfire.

Throw up stories are hilarious, but we're not really talking about physical illness. Doing life together in a way that is rich and meaningful means that we get to be there for the celebratory, joyous times, but also for the hard parts. And the gross parts. It means that sometimes, we'll experience one another as the best versions of ourselves. And sometimes as the worst. And even the healthiest of us get sick sometimes. Maybe you're supporting one of your people during a difficult season right now, and it's exhausting. Or maybe, in this moment, one of your people is holding your hair back for you while you lean over the bowl.

We need to know who our people are; who are the ones that we are supposed to walk with and do life with on this level? Of course we desire to be kind, loving, and gracious to all people, but let's be honest. There are a select few whom I would invite or allow into those truly raw and awful moments. Throwing up in front of someone is humbling because you simply cannot control the ghastly sounds coming out of you. And holding back the hair of someone who is ill, being in such close proximity to their vomit, is an assault on all senses. Both require a level of intimacy and safety that you simply cannot (and would not want to) share with everyone.

Sometimes committing to this level of intimacy means listening to your friend retell the demise of her marriage for the eight-thousandth time. Sometimes it's my person listening patiently to me as I try to figure out why I feel worried (again). Sometimes it looks like showing up with snacks and red wine. Sometimes it's sending your new-mom friend to bed while you pace the floor with her crying baby.

Sometimes it means crawling into your person's darkness with them and just being quietly present. Sometimes it means sticking around at the hospital, or police station, or funeral home. Sometimes it looks like laying in your child's bed with them, well past their bedtime (and well into grown-up time) as they open up their heart and say the things they are unable to say in daylight. Sometimes it means letting your person safely spew negativity and poison, without shaming them for being sick, knowing that once they've finished, they'll feel better and will be able to see more clearly. And then—the hard part—letting them off the hook for all of the ridiculous, paranoid ideas they held true the day before. Being present when someone vomits can mean that you end up caught in the cross-fire of something that has nothing to do with you, but you're the *safe person* who bears the brunt ... or *your* safe person bears the brunt for you.

We don't always do it well. You don't. I don't. Because we're humans, sometimes we recoil in disgust. We run from pain. We make judgements on how others navigate their hard seasons. We tire of negativity. Our empathy short circuits. We don't listen for the whole story. We lose sight of the fact that, often, people aren't just being arseholes (my sweet grandmother's word) for no reason. We forget that it is an honor to hold space for our people and carry their stories. When this happens, we desert our people when they most need us to offer comfort, solace, and a cool cloth. There is no judgement and no shame for this. We have all let our people down at one point or another. What's beautiful is that we can simply begin again; we can start over right now. We can step in close, hold back hair, and whisper words of comfort.

This is love, friends. Relationships that mean something can bear the weight of a heavy soul. (I am not talking about toxic or abusive relationships; that's a different conversation). The only option for those who will not endure the smell of vomit, or who refuse to handle the occasional mess, is to do life alone. And I would argue, then, that the word *life* would need to be substituted with something much more meager, sad, and one-dimensional.

For me, the choice is easy. I'm choosing to do life with my people in a way that is rich and meaningful. I am fully in: for the tears and the parties, for the worst and best versions, in sickness and in health. The only thing I cannot promise is that your *actual* barfing won't make me laugh because, like I said, that is how these situations affect me.

Chapter 17

Learning the Hard Way

"Nothing ever goes away until it teaches us what we need to know."
PEMA CHÖDRÖN

A bunch of years ago, we put a three-story addition on our home. When the builders dug down for the new foundation, it produced a temporary dirt mountain that was a dream come true for my kids. In the span of hours, that dirt mountain transformed into something spectacular! It was home to several Tonka trucks, diggers, My Little Ponies, and Hot Wheels cars. It was covered in elaborate road systems. It had villages and caves, horse pastures and "sand" castles. Our dirt mountain provided many hours of entertainment.

One day, I went outside to find my, then, 4-year old daughter and 6-year old son standing on a wooden toboggan at the summit of our dirt mountain. I watched, frozen, as my precious babes stood, one behind the other, legs braced, both hanging on to the rope (because "safety first!") and began scooching themselves forward.

My initial inclination was to yell *"Stop!"* and rush up the mountain to their rescue. They clearly needed to be bubble-wrapped for their own protection. Instead, I took a deep breath and calmly asked myself,

In this situation, is good parenting rushing in to save them from possible injury, or is good parenting letting them be adventurous, figuring out on their own that this standing-toboggan-ride likely won't end well?

Realizing they probably wouldn't die, I bit my tongue and watched them descend. It was a rough ride, but there were no broken bones. Reflecting afterwards on their maiden voyage, they came to the consensus that once was enough. They learned from their experience. And possibly even better, they began the process of learning to trust themselves.

Learning that is meaningful usually involves making mistakes and getting dirty. Regrettably, we oftentimes short-circuit authentic learning by relying on the "Coles Notes" (Cliffs, if you're American) instead of reading the whole book. We offer *cheat sheets* to our kids, our friends, and even to ourselves. "For their own good" (we think), we want to control information, and situations, and choices in order to avoid mis-steps and unpleasant outcomes.

Our intentions are loving. Armed with our deeply-held beliefs and our heightened 20/20 hindsight, we want to save one another from hardship and heartache by providing shortcuts and life hacks that reveal the best way forward. And while we certainly *do* want to learn from the experience and wise counsel of others, it's difficult to really *own* something until we've wrestled with it ourselves.

Blind acceptance doesn't allow for authentic understanding. External motivation may offer immediate results, but the results don't tend to be lasting. Separation from apron strings, following the road less traveled, wrestling internally, discovering for one's self—these intrinsically motivated discoveries, that can sometimes look like "straying from the path," may actually have more staying power.

With our own children, there are phases of parenting where we provide black and white rules, and enforce consequences so that they'll be safe and learn how to act appropriately. But as our children mature, extrinsic rewards are no longer sufficient; sometimes we have to let them figure it out. We continue to provide boundaries and wise counsel, while also recognizing that they need to experience and learn for themselves in order for the roots of understanding to be profound, far-reaching, and hardy.

Trial and error, multiple failures, and re-vamped *editions* are often a necessary part of the process toward becoming whole, authentic people. This applies to becoming fully who we were created to be, to discovering our talents, to honing our skills, to refining our characters, to finding the right path, to making a discovery, and even to embracing personal faith.

When I began journeying toward authenticity in my early twenties, I was somewhat cavalier, sometimes inadvertently offensive, and definitely not smooth. It was a rough ride down the dirt mountain, but it was allowed. God knew I had something to learn about navigating being real and discovering my true self. And I *did* learn it. But not without a few wipeouts along the way.

I've never done 'neutral' very well. I can formulate opinions on the fly, muster passion for just about anything, and expostulate in such a way that others may perceive me in ways I did not foresee or intend.

When I first felt the call to be 'real,' I leaned into it enthusiastically, not realizing yet that others might not enjoy my candor. I intentionally chose to make myself vulnerable, sometimes with the wrong people. I was expressive with my thoughts and opinions without thinking through how I might be interpreted.

I've explained before that I see most ideas, situations, and feelings in pictures and metaphors. This can lend a very visual component to my words that might work well for writing but can sometimes make my spoken words sound extreme.

One such occurrence that makes me cringe and laugh loudly to this day illustrates the point. In my early twenties, while volunteering my time with youth, I once prayed passionately ... aloud ... in a large group ... that God would "remove the religious poles from peoples' butts." Mmhmm. You can already imagine how this went wrong. While I was envisioning something like scarecrows—fixed in place by nature of the poles, unmoving, no autonomy—and was using the metaphor to pray for freedom and grace, others were picturing something quite graphic and unpleasant. Oops. Thankfully, it was before the days of viral tweets or the damage might have been far worse. As it was, people were offended, pissed off, and I was mortified.

I'd like to tell you that I learned to perfectly temper my words after that first descent down the dirt mountain, that no offensive thing ever exited my mouth from that time forward, and that my words were never mis-interpreted again. But, it *did* happen again. And again.

In fact, recently, a friend laughingly told me that I talk about punching people in the face *a lot*. Startled, I realized that I *do* say that a lot, though I sometimes modify it to involve a throat punch. I am not a violent person in the least—for me, it's all metaphor and humor—but based only on my word choice, I can understand how others (especially those who don't know me well) might question whether I have a serious problem with aggression. So, yes, I'm still learning to temper my words.

Throughout the years, Love has continued to provide wise counsel but has never forced me to get off the toboggan. The result, over time, is that I have learned to discern what is mine to own and modify versus what is on others to deal with, because their offense is the result of something in them. I've figured out how to hold in tension living freely and honestly *and* living with sensitivity for those with differing world views. I've had to learn to walk the very fine line between paranoia (worrying constantly about others' perceptions of me) and living from a place of love (caring enough for people to choose the kind response).

Two decades have passed since those early years of learning to be real. Love has allowed me to experiment, to test, to falter and, sometimes, to fail miserably. Even when others tried to manage me, God did not bubble-wrap me or impose a strict code. Just as we don't want our kids to act a certain way because they're afraid of us, or to hang out with us because we *make* them, neither does God force us. No one wants programmable robots.

Instead of external control in the form of law, grace is what allowed me to become the "me" I was intended to be (a process that is ongoing...clearly). Love's kindness and forgiveness gave me space to learn how to walk in a way that was deeply real. No one was compelling me to act a certain way. No one was forcing me to adhere to a prescribed path. I embraced with joy who I'd been created to be and engaged with life as myself.

Love offers us the space to figure it all out. Our character is refined using real life situations. We learn what we're made of through hard lessons. We seek out the divine because we realize we *want* to, not because our parents or some other influencer told us we must. We learn to trust ourselves, knowing that Love in us is trustworthy. Our understanding becomes authentic and our learning meaningful.

For this to happen, it usually means learning the hard way ... and maybe a risky trip or two down a dirt mountain.

Chapter 18

Understanding and Being Understood

---

*"The most basic of all human needs is the need
to understand and be understood."*

RALPH NICHOLS

My thought process began from within the confines of a staff bathroom stall where inspirational literature is often photocopied and taped haphazardly at toilet-eye-level to the interior of the stall door. The gist of the particular piece was that with words as our primary vehicle for communication, one would think we'd be better at it. But we're not. Most over-talk and under-listen. Facing the stall door, I was told again that less is more when it comes to communication. Apparently, fewer words is the way to go.

While I'm certain the Covey-esque message was intended to encourage, "two ears, one mouth" rang loudly in my head—that adorable little saying that has been hurting the feelings of the chatty since ... forever. Needing to be understood and listening to understand are often positioned as opposites. Immature versus mature. Self-centered versus selfless. Discourteous versus well-mannered. It seems we subtly applaud those who process internally as thoughtful, while shaking our heads disdainfully at those more inclined to verbal processing. Juxtaposed, we can almost feel the tension mounting—two entities facing off against one another. One is active, desperate to ensure the listener really gets them. And the other is passive, silent and resigned, gracious enough to let the other speak but maybe not courageous enough to honor his or her or their own voice.

But why? Why, so often, do we pit these two against one another like they're dichotomies or extremes or mortal enemies? Certainly some personality types experience the need to be understood more intensely than others, but all humans feel it, because being understood makes us feel known. The psychological need to be known and understood is a close second to our physical need for food, water, shelter and safety. As I've held these seemingly repelling forces in separate fists, I've become aware of their concurrent need to pull together. Though they are different, they are woven together at a visceral level— two sides of the same coin. We cannot be known and understood without opening our mouths to communicate. And we cannot know and understand others without closing our mouths to listen. As it turns out, it's both-and. The question is, where are we on the continuum? Do we need to talk more or listen more?

We all have that 'friend' who drones on and on, never pausing for breath, never leaving an opening for interjection or response. (Small pause for nervous self-reflection: *oh god, don't let it be me!*). For me, the desire to be understood can make me talk way too much. It makes me keep going, long after the point has been made, desperate to secure the listener's understanding. When we live from this end of the continuum, a healthy tennis game of speaking and listening becomes a solo event of talking and waiting to speak. People who don't listen are challenging.

You know what else is challenging? People who don't talk. Friendships with people who are "all listening-no talking" tend to fade quite quickly for me. Not only do I want to be known, I want to know people. When I share my thoughts and ideas and there is zero reciprocation, it can leave me feeling unnerved, maybe even a little paranoid. A more quiet personality may be a genuinely excellent listener. Or they may not care a sniff about what you're saying and, while they're not interrupting, neither are they engaged or interested. Or maybe they have felt rejected, ignored, and not understood themselves to the point of despondency and resignation to silence. Less talking doesn't necessarily equate to good listening.

This is absolutely an *everything in moderation* situation. When everyone speaks and no one listens, it's chaos. But when everyone listens and no one speaks, it's a graveyard. Maturity is holding these two things in tension and allowing the pendulum to rest somewhere between blabbermouth and mute. In other words, knowing when to speak up and when to shut up. But even with healthy communication in place, humans are imperfect. The true antidote to feeling misunderstood—or conversely, the way to live fully known—*is* to listen. But not just to any old voice.

What if we transfer the listening to understand part to God? What if we remove it from the natural realm of human interaction to the seeking of Love's perspective and wise counsel? The desire to feel understood is requited when I seek the one who embodies understanding. I was rude to the God of the universe for years! I was that ignorant friend who would blather on ad nauseam—talking, processing, questioning, seeking wisdom—but leaving no space for response. It's like I would pick up the telephone, go full-stream-of-consciousness-running-monologue, and then hang up. Until I was taught to be quiet. God would talk and I would listen—to stories about how I was made, who I was created to be, what I was called to, and how I am so loved beyond measure.

By listening, I began to live as one who is known and loved. When we understand who Love says we are, it diminishes our need to be understood by everyone else. This is not license to act like petulant children, abdicating common decency and scorning the counsel of others—"God says I'm awesome, so I don't care what you think!" We are created for connection, not only with the divine, but with one another. However, when we are comfortable and secure in our identity, it reduces our need to explain ourselves incessantly. Though we have an innate human longing to feel understood, when we live from a place of being understood and known by Love, it lessens the desperation and urgent need to be understood by others. It becomes the icing on the cake and not the cake itself.

Let's quiet ourselves and listen. To the one who lovingly designed us. To the one who calls us by name. To the one who knows us completely. When we live as those who are loved and known, the pendulum comes to rest.

The way to feel understood is to listen to understand.

It's not one or the other, friends. It's both-and.

Chapter 19

Forgive Me?

"Resentment is like drinking poison and expecting the other person to die."

AUTHOR UNKNOWN

Years ago, I was asked to speak on forgiveness at a women's retreat. I carefully crafted the most beautiful teaching—a compilation of all the best resources I could find. And while it was a well-written document, because I had referenced other peoples' ideas, adding none of my own, something was missing. It lacked authenticity. Regurgitating scripts from my church upbringing, as well as stories told by others, allowed me a degree of separation from my own experience. My own unpolished voice and gritty examples were conspicuously absent. Forgiveness was easy to talk about when it was disembodied from my own painful examples.

A few days before I was to speak, I felt challenged to scrap it and write from my own experience. I erased the whole thing and started over. Worst. Nightmare. In the aftermath, I was thankful for the pressure-cooker-experience that forced me to gather my *own* thoughts, thus articulating my evolving understanding of forgiveness.

Though it's absurd to even attempt to capture an idea of such magnitude and meaning in a few short paragraphs, my hope, at the very least, is to convey its immense importance for those who desire to live fully.

We humans talk about forgiveness a lot. We know we're supposed to do it; we even *want* to do it. But in spite of this, we're not actually very good at it. We say the words, we act it out, we make our kids act it out, but often, it's not an authentic experience. We say, "Sorry!" and rattle off the script like little parrots, without any real sense of remorse or reconciliation or relief. Or we use it as a means of bypassing important and difficult work.

The topic of forgiveness does the seemingly impossible in that it straddles the worlds of pop culture and ancient religion. While it's certainly a tenet of most religions, if you google "forgiveness," you'll also find posts from Psychology Today, the Mayo Clinic, Oprah, and more. But it's more than a trendy buzz word; it's a grueling and necessary act of will that cannot (and should not!) be forced on us or done for us.

So, what is it? Why should I forgive? What does it matter if I harbor unforgiveness (which is a neologism, not a real word, but we're using it anyway) or resentment toward you? I'm not hurting anyone by carrying around this hurt, this grudge, this anger. Yeah, you are! You're hurting *you*.

No one can strong-arm us into forgiveness; we have to choose it. We don't have to feel like it, we don't have to like what happened, we don't even have to be *over* what happened. We may not feel immediate relief as a result of speaking the words, but in the intentional choosing, we can, like Wikipedia says, "undergo a change in feelings and attitude regarding an offense, let go of negative emotions such as vengefulness ... and [experience] an increased ability to wish the offender well."[1] The alternative—deciding to ignore, bury or just move on—while omissive, is also a choice; a choice that doesn't necessarily produce life.

Friends, I don't want to scare you, but zombies are real! They're the ones who wander around in this life, dead inside. No heartbeat. No life in their eyes. They don't experience the joy or fullness of life that is ours for the living. Pain and unforgiveness can render us shells; shadows of the people we were created to be. I don't know about you, but I have zero interest in being the living dead.

Each time we avoid dealing with pain and brokenness, we close doors. When we refuse to reconcile with others or ourselves, we essentially close off rooms in our "house" until all of a sudden, we realize we are living in a very small space. No thanks. As much as is possible for us, let's shove open the windows and fling wide the doors. Forgiveness is a huge part of living in your whole house.

We are imperfect humans living in an imperfect world, and sooner or later (probably sooner, like every. single. day.), we are going to be mistreated, hurt, left out, and wounded. The pain will likely be inflicted by someone you know, respect, and love—maybe a family member, a lover, a close friend, a colleague, or someone who you think should know better. Sometimes we wonder how a person so close to us could hurt us like this? But it actually makes sense; we're more vulnerable with those we love and trust. It's almost easier to let a stranger off the hook than someone we know. Though I might feel angry in the moment when that *freaking moron!* cuts me off on the highway, the anger flares, and then it burns out. But from a trusted person, the pain cuts deeply.

Sometimes we get selective memory when we talk about forgiveness. That is, we tend to remember only the ways in which we've been wronged. Instead of getting blamey and sucked down the sink hole of self-pity, let's remember that just as we've been hurt *by* others, we have, also, knowingly or unknowingly inflicted pain. This is why we need to understand how to ask for forgiveness *and* how to extend forgiveness.

Permission to speak honestly? Though in theory, it may be in our best interest to forgive, in practice, it's not always so simple. Moving toward healing can be brutally onerous when there has been an absence of process, or no owning of the errors. Or horrific, undeserving plotlines have unfolded. Sometimes the circumstance, such as not having access to the full truth of a trauma, is a legitimate hindrance in the process of forgiveness.

Though many will align in the basic belief that forgiveness is integral, we must take care not to force, by-pass, bully, or overly simplify the process. Sometimes being mandated to forgive is actually harmful. Shaming a person who is wrestling to be released from the enduring effects of violence or abuse or trauma is not loving. "Speaking the truth in love" that God won't forgive you if you don't forgive is spiritual abuse. We need to ensure that people on the journey toward forgiveness are not told they are the problem. No victimizing the victim. (Thanks for listening to my Tedtalk).

Forgiveness is good for us. The purpose of forgiveness is *not* so that we can be *nice* people or weak people who tow the line and strive to get along. The purpose of forgiveness is not that we resign ourselves to doormat-dom. Extending forgiveness to others (*and* ourselves) and accepting forgiveness from them (*and* ourselves) is what allows us to live fully and whole-heartedly.

The benefits of forgiveness are not only mental, emotional, and spiritual, but physical. Karen Swartz, M.D. at The Johns Hopkins Hospital, says, "There is an enormous physical burden to being hurt and disappointed ... Chronic anger puts you into a fight-or-flight mode, which results in numerous changes in heart rate, blood pressure and immune response. Those changes, then, increase the risk of depression, heart disease and diabetes, among other conditions. Forgiveness, however, calms stress levels, leading to improved health."[3]

Forgiveness is an act of agency. Those few words, whispered courageously through hurt and tears, "I forgive you," have massive repercussions for bitterness and brokenness. We have to act offensively. It is not always possible to wait for reciprocation, reconciliation, or change of heart on the part of the person or people. It's wonderful and validating when it happens that way, but there are no guarantees that it will.

Whether spoken to an actual person or aloud to the night sky, we can proclaim forgiveness. And when we do, we advance into enemy-controlled territory and we take back ground that has been stolen. The walls that have been built, the silence that has lingered, the separation and division and brokenness in relationships … this can all be healed with humble hearts and simple words. Simple, but warrior-like. *Will you forgive me? I forgive you.* When we forgive, we are turning toward health, and brokenness loses its grip.

When we forgive, we let go of the offense and decide not to punish the offender, even if they deserve it. In *normal* circumstances, as in, those that do not involve abuse, it means that we not only pardon the person who has wronged us, but also accept and restore them to relationship. For example, when our children have acted inappropriately and we've dealt with it, we don't keep bringing it up, referencing it, reminding them about their screw-ups, or rubbing their noses in it (even when we'd really like to).

Just as it's important to understand what forgiveness is, it's as important to understand what it is *not*.

Forgiveness is not saying "it's okay." Many of us have been hesitant to forgive because we've faultily understood *I forgive you* to mean *what you did is okay*. Nope. What you did is *not* okay, but I'm letting it go. I'm not going to carry it anymore.

To help my students understand, I explain that we are all wearing backpacks. As hard things happen, it's as though rocks are placed into our backpacks. If we don't stop from time to time and remove the heavy rocks, we will be hindered in everything we do. Carrying around those heavy, hard things does not serve us well.

Forgiveness is not an invitation or requirement to stay in an unhealthy situation. I can completely forgive someone for a wrong done, but if there are no positive changes, it does not always mean that I continue to be in relationship with that person or people. *(Hopefully, it does mean that I can actually see them at the grocery store without wanting to ram my cart into their legs.)*

Forgiveness is not a passive aggressive or white-washed means of informing someone that you've been angry or resentful. It is not an attack cloaked in goodness. I can't tell you how many times I've had people approach me with "I need to ask you for forgiveness because I've been really resenting you for … " It wasn't about something I had done and, truly, it had nothing to do with me. We need to check our motivation. We might feel released and validated in our pain, but now we've slimed someone. Sometimes forgiveness doesn't involve another person. It is worked out within yourself, because it's actually about you.

Forgiveness is not a magic pill. My friend, Steve, shares honestly that in his experience, choosing forgiveness does not take away the pain. It does not prove to be the ibuprofen or surgery that masks or removes the hurt. At all. He acknowledges that while it can remove resentment, the desire for vengeance, and that it can aid with moving forward in life, in some ways, it seems like a Utopian idea; that it's advertised as a magic pill that is supposed to heal the effects of wrongs done. But doesn't necessarily deliver. The healing we seek will be more probable with the inclusion of self-care, boundary-setting, counseling, truth-searching and telling, and falling into the arms of safe friends and family. Administering the pill of forgiveness is only part of the overall care package for the hurt person.

Forgiveness is not weakness. It means you are strong. In our culture, people feel they need to stick up for their rights. Don't take less than you are owed! Make them pay for what they did! We equate forgiving with being a sucker. If someone owes you and they refuse to pay, they are certainly in the wrong. They should pay. But what if you *choose* to let it go, not because you want to avoid conflict, but so that the debt no longer has a hold on you? This isn't always the right thing—sometimes full reconciliation does need to happen—but sometimes it *is* the right thing.

I honestly don't know if forgiveness comes naturally to humans, and there are supporting arguments for both sides. Regardless, there are certain personality types that seem to have an easier time of it. More often than not, though, I believe it must be modeled and practiced—a learned behavior.

Growing up, there was *a lot* of forgiving to be done in my family. Four kids, born every two years or so, can be simultaneously the best of friends and the worst of enemies. I give all credit to my mother for teaching us how to forgive. Though we balked and resisted the process, she made us walk it out as often as was needed. Which was a lot.

When an issue occurred, we weren't allowed to simply ream off a snarky "Sorry!" in our best dismissive *I-didn't-really-do-it-but-I-want-this-to-be-over-now-so-I'll-just-say-it* voice. My mom taught us to own our part. She taught us the script: "I'm sorry I _____ . Will you forgive me?" "Yes, I forgive you." And then, the hug.

This practice, over and over and over, embedded the process in my psyche. No longer a script, it became rails to run on. This process, learned almost by rote, has stayed with me. I've applied it my entire life, and it's helped to navigate bumps in relationships with friends, colleagues, and partners. It's a gift I've been able to pass on to my own children, not to mention to classrooms full of students each year.

If we desire to live fully—to be healthy people, physically, spiritually, mentally, and emotionally—we need to lighten our backpacks. We need to let go of offenses. We need to forgive. Whether it's something done to us, like a broken confidence or unfaithfulness, or something that was *not* done, like the withholding of care and affirmation, we can live free.

It will cost you something. But it will be worth it.

Chapter 20

Why You Need "Baby Group"

"Good company in a journey makes the way seem shorter."
IZAAK WALTON

You need "Baby Group," and I'm gonna tell you why. This is more of a story than a lesson, but in the journey toward wholeness and being the best version of myself, this group of women must be acknowledged and honored. You can insert whatever terms you need to replace "Baby Group." Maybe for you it's your AA group, a house church, dinner club, or your hockey team. The point is, we need other people in our journey.

My preference is hand-crafted, artisan jewelry—not expensive, just unique. I like to wear original pieces that no one else owns, but I break this rule for a charm bracelet that is also worn by eight other women. It holds a place of honor on my wrist, and I wear it almost every single day—not because it's beautiful, but because it's symbolic of the women who gave it to me: my baby group.

I love my baby group. I *need* my baby group. I should probably mention that there are, in fact, no babies in our baby group. Actually, there aren't even that many kids because most of the babies are now 'tweens and teenagers. And, truthfully, they are not even *invited* to baby group most of the time—it has become a moms-only thing. We made numerous attempts to rebrand as "Moms' Night Out" or "The Muffin Tops" (because … never mind … you know why), but it never really stuck. So baby group it is.

Baby group began with two of us who invited another one, who invited her friend, who invited a colleague from work, who invited her neighbor, and so on. Before we knew it, we were a thriving group of moms and babies.

In Canada, we are blessed to have a year of paid(ish) maternity leave, so for a whole year, we met *at least* once a week, but more often than not, two to three times a week. It was our saving grace during a time when our worlds had completely changed, when we were raw with lack of sleep and were constantly wondering what was normal.

Am I okay? Is my baby okay? Is my marriage okay? Am I losing my mind? Am I doing a good job? Am I still me?

We carried on meeting as often as we could, even after many of us had returned to work. Second rounds of babies were born, and then for some, thirds and fourths, rendering our meetings a little chaotic. Some of the connections drifted—not for sinister reasons, but simply due to schedule differences and busy lives. Some of us, however, were not ready to say goodbye and our core group became a stable nine.

The interesting thing about our baby group is that many of us would never have crossed paths without babies as the common denominator. We came from different backgrounds, different professions, different physical locations, and different belief structures. What we had in common was that our babies were born at around the same time. What we had in common was that we needed this support network to help navigate parenthood. What we had in common is that we were not interested in faking it.

And so, this initially unlikely group of women became friends. Not superficial, fluffy friends—but true, safe, visceral, gut level, raw, honest friends.

I see the formation of relationships like a living entity that is being knitted together and created. Every interaction shared—whether the discussion of a great recipe, or the honest admission that someone is feeling really low—all of these create lines of connection, passing a ball of wool from one to another, until something resembling an intricate web is formed.

When I look back to the beginning of baby group, in my mind's eye, I can picture us standing in a circle, passing this ball of fine wool or thread between us. Every conversation, every tear, every outbreak of uncontrollable laughter, every funny story, every breast pad discreetly tucked away and then accidentally left behind in couch cushions, every shared insight, every frustrated vent of anger, every word of wisdom and experience, every cup of coffee poured. All of these were like fine threads, not necessarily strong as individual filaments, but wound together and tossed back and forth millions of times, they developed into something hardy.

Early on, I'm sure there were gaps and spaces in our web where, maybe, we worried about precious things falling though—*Is my honesty safe here? Can I really say this out loud?*—but with enough time spent and the continued passing of the ball, the web became something substantial that could hold heavy and precious things.

It's a messy, beautiful web of connection that has required an investment of time, truth, honesty, listening, and sharing. It didn't just happen. It was intentional.

These ladies are my people. I love them and I trust them. Together, we have navigated, and continue to navigate, the highs and lows of life. We've hashed out our parenting joys and woes at every age and stage. We have prayed for and waited alongside one another for successful adoptions. We have cried together when marriages ended. We have rooted for one another in infertility. We have grieved the loss of babies. We have grieved the loss of parents. We have celebrated remarriage. We have conferred on sex, make up, menstrual cycles, paint colors, spouses, and packing lunches. We still ask: Am I okay? Is my kid okay? Is my marriage okay? Am I losing my mind? Am I doing a good job? Am I still me? We have had 'girls only' weekends away, family trips together, thousands of play dates, and huge family parties that are *always* a gong show and *always* worth it.

Our kids know one another. Even those who aren't close friends (though many of them are) know "that kid is a baby group kid." They seem to sense that they're related somehow. And in my mind, they are.

Our baby group sessions (sans kids, of course) are not quiet, reserved, "proper" gatherings. There is a lot of talking and too much food. There are usually Hello Dolly squares, lots of cheese, wine, and whatever sad gluten-free baking I've brought with me. Sometimes we talk all at once and over top of one another. At other times, we jump in and out of the many strands of concurrent conversation. But often, we listen intently to one person, without interruption, as she pours out her hurt or worry or frustration. We've all had our turns in this chair. We listen and offer support. We say, "We get it. We understand."

We had baby group a few nights ago. Like always, we got all caught up on the latest celebrations and concerns. And like always, we left feeling like we might be normal—and like our kids might be normal, too. The next morning, one of the mamas wrote, via group text: "I always feel more hopeful the morning after baby group."

And that is exactly it. Solidarity. Baby group only works if all the members are authentic and honest. If members can't share their questions and failures and darkest angst for fear of being judged or shamed, then all benefit is lost. The last thing any of us need is to feel that sense of competition with one another. In our group, we can brag about our kids' awesome moments, and the group celebrates with you. We can also send out a group text lamenting that our child is *for sure* going to end up in jail (or we are!), and there's nothing that can be done, so just cry with me.

What began in the early days as two to three times a week eventually spread to once a month. And now, because our babies lead such busy lives, it's often much longer than that. But lapses of time do not diminish the safety and affection.

Many of us don't see one another on a regular basis during this ridiculously busy phase of life (*sorry, younger moms—it doesn't get easier, it gets different*), but I know these women are there, solid ground underneath it all. Getting together with my baby group feels like rest in the midst of treading water. It allows me to touch down for a moment, knowing my feet will land on something solid. We remind one another that the water isn't as deep or as dark as it sometimes seems. We remind one another that we're not alone.

You need a "baby group," so gather some people. You don't have to have everything in common. You don't even need to have kids. Start sharing stories, holding confidences, telling the truth, and being a safe place. Pass the ball of yarn back and forth between the two of you, or three of you, or ten of you. Do it on purpose. The intricate web that forms will be a thing of beauty.

Chapter 21

Lessons From Nan

"I've learned that people will forget what you said, people will forget what you did, but people will never forget how you made them feel"
MAYA ANGELOU

To varying degrees, we *all* want to leave our mark; to be impactful with our lives. At its worst, this can look cut throat and desperate. It can look like self-promotion and unhealthy competition. At its best, it looks like self-actualized humans running in their own lanes and living as healthy versions of themselves, rising to become who they were created to be.

As one who longs for meaning, the thought of wasting this one life I have to live here on earth—whether by laziness or by focusing on the wrong things—is the most dismal of thoughts. I want to leave a legacy that points to the important things. But figuring out what's truly important can take a little time.

End of life musings get shared around occasionally, like "At the end of your life, no one says, *Oh man, I wish I'd worked more.*" These citations can feel a little trite out of context *or* they can serve to refocus our frenzied efforts. The point is, when we mistakenly ascribe more value than warranted to the things deemed important by society, we can end up spending our one life proving ourselves and potentially missing the *most* important things.

Lest there be misunderstanding, I should restate that I'm the exact opposite of laissez-faire. Though I've mellowed with age, I am as driven and Type-A as they come. I place a very high value on education. I want to provide financially for my family. I want to be known as someone who did something with her life. If you're called to it, there is nothing wrong with ascending the corporate ladder, excelling in your field, getting a publishing deal, winning the gold medal. But what if these are meant to be the side benefits of those living their fullest lives? What if they're not actually the targets?

When the desire for meaning or legacy disintegrates into unhealthy places, it becomes misguided and ends up looking more like lust for success and notoriety. Success as a bi-product of hard work and excellence is deserving; however, the desire for success as an end goal, in and of itself, will have us all wrapped up in knots, working too hard, striving, pushing, and hustling. All so that there is something to show for our time here on Earth. To demonstrate we were meaningful. To prove we mattered.

My youthful ambitions have been shored up with an understanding that there are more significant monuments to leave behind—things that don't get framed and hung on a wall. Things that don't get displayed on a mantle or in a trophy cabinet. Things that don't make the New York Times best seller list.

Last week, I had the immeasurable honor of being with my grandmother as she left this earth. It's had me really thinking about the measure of a life: *how do we measure our meaning?* I think my Nan may have been on to something.

My Nan was born in a small, rural community in 1922. The second youngest of twelve siblings, she began and finished her public education, from 1st through 8th grade, in the same one-room school-house that her father and grandfather had also attended, and that her own children would eventually attend. She didn't leave her small community. She didn't attend university. She didn't invent anything. She didn't have letters and accreditations after her name. She didn't have a large bank account. She was not famous beyond her family and friends. She didn't leave an anthology of work—at least not one that was visible.

But my relatively unknown grandmother left a notable legacy for those of us who were blessed to have her in our lives. She endowed us with invaluable gifts.

Nan gave us the gift of family.

I didn't realize how extraordinary it was to have a strong family connection until I was an adult. I simply thought all families were like mine. My Nan established rhythms for gathering that forged strong, enduring ties. We have gathered regularly our whole lives for Boxing Day, Easter, Mother's Day, family birthdays, Thanksgiving, summers at the camp, and more.

It's always a *loud crowd*, all talking simultaneously, laughing uproariously, gorging on delicious food, and loving one another well. And this many years later, we still gather. We have logged so much time together. We really know, and like, and love one another. And I credit my Nan for this.

Nan gave us the gift of safety.

Growing up, she was woven through the fabric of our lives. She was not a distant relation but almost a pseudo-parent, a safe person.

I have a vivid early memory of Nan arriving on our doorstep unan-nounced, having driven many hours from another province. My mom was pregnant with my youngest sister and so ill she couldn't get out of bed. Five-year-old Ellen was pouring bowls of dry Cheerios for her two younger siblings when suddenly, the door opened and in walked my Nan. She had a feeling we needed her, so she showed up. I remember the incredible relief and safety of her presence.

As we got older, all of the grandchildren, individually, spent large amounts of time with our Nan—suppers together, short visits over cups of tea, naps on her couch, and even weekend sleepovers. Whether planned ahead or a spontaneous stop-in, she was overjoyed to see us. Being with her felt like exhaling. We never felt like an interruption or a bother. We knew we'd be welcomed into her safe harbor.

Nan gave us the gift of time.

One of Nan's greatest gifts was her time. In a world that is rushed and busy, she would make a pot of tea. In the frenzy of life, she'd invite you to sit at the table to talk or play games. She could chat light-heartedly or listen while you poured out your sorry, confused heart. She had time.

My brother says that Nan could always engage us where we were, whether with wisdom and comfort, or just by being together. She was aware of everything going on in the world and could converse for hours about history, current news, how things might play out in the future, and her memories of technologies as they had unfolded during her lifetime. She always had time and made us feel like the most important people in the world.

She gave us the gift of a spiritual heritage.

Whether by sharing her devotional readings with us or our simple observation of her as she lived a life of faith and resiliency, even during very difficult things, she modeled a life of trusting God.

She invested greatly in the spiritual formation of her grandkids, teaching us scripture and giving us a road map for our Bibles through what she called "sword drills." At the end of each sword drill week, she'd create a "fishpond" to reward those of us who had committed our memory verses to heart. We'd pull a string to find money attached at the other end. It was a total bribe..and it totally worked!

Nan gave us the gift of memories.

We had our Nan a long time—far longer than most—and as a result, we are rich with memories. There are certain smells that will forever remind me of Nan. The wild roses in her yard, the smell of geraniums in her porch, fresh bread, and the wood smoke from her old kitchen stove, or the pot-belly stove down at the cottage that we called "the camp."

The kettle boiled and cups of tea were poured. I drank tea with milk and sugar long after I'd stopped taking sugar in my tea. It was how she'd always served it, so it tasted like Nan's house. And there was always something sweet to accompany your tea. Homemade bread and rolls with strawberry jam tasted like Nan's house. So did Apple Crisp and crushed up potato chips on casseroles.

Down at the camp, she provided her grandkids with old dishes to use in our forest playhouse. I'm not sure what *you* used, but *we* had china tea cups and plates for *our* mud pies! Most of us remember clearly the sound of her two-fingered whistle through the woods, indicating that supper was ready.

When she still had her eyesight, she knitted fourteen pairs of mittens every winter to keep her grandkids warm. She hid Easter eggs so well for our hunt each year that we would still be finding them six months later.

And finally, we will always remember her standing in her front living room window to wave good-bye as we drove away. Every single time.

These are all such simple things, and yet, they are what I remember. They are what feels meaningful.

Let's rethink what it means to matter. While my desire is to live to my full potential and to walk courageously the path that has been set for *me*, I don't want to be tricked or distracted into pursuing the lesser things that seem like the bigger things.

Maya Angelou's words at the beginning of this chapter give me pause, as they say, because I haven't always done this well. My personality leans hard in the direction of *rushy* efficiency, over-achievement, speed, and accuracy. This thought regularly reminds me to slow down.

If, at the end of my days, no one remembers anything I said, and there is nothing to show for my efforts, but *my people* rise and call me blessed—thankful that I taught them the value of family, thankful that I made them feel safe, thankful that I had time for them, thankful that I introduced them to faith, thankful for rich, loving memories—that will be enough. I will be *well* satisfied.

However, if they also want to award me a trophy for it, I won't say no. I'll graciously accept, thanking God and my manager. I'm still me, after all.

Chapter 22

Keeping It Real II

My kids fight *all the time*. As a teacher, I'm fairly skilled in employing self-control and patience, but when my own kids fight, it pushes me *right. over. the. flipping. edge*. It looks a little bit like this: patience (I am *so* God's gift to motherhood), paatience (umm, this is getting annoying), paaatience (gritting teeth), paaaaaatience (closing cupboard doors with all my strength), and ... *freak out*! I find it's really effective parenting when you yell at your kids to stop yelling at each other. Haha. Kidding. Nope, not really kidding. Some days I feel like I'm rocking it, and on others, I'm so rocked.

✳

This next one is really vulnerable for me to share, so please hold these pearls tenderly. Seeing a mom with a brood of kids, as in four or five, gives me little pangs in my heart. I am *so* very content and thankful for my children (and have to trust that God knew my spicy two would be enough for me), but I always believed I'd have a large family. It just didn't work out that way.

✳

Being me is a perpetual dilemma. People often believe me to be an extrovert because of how I present in public; I am social and confident. I truly enjoy people and I want everyone to feel included. However,

I am actually equally introverted/extroverted. Right in the middle. A so-called ambivert. This leaves me in incredible inner turmoil most of the time. My extrovert loves parties and social gatherings and she fist-pumps at an invitation to hang out with people ... it seems like the *best* idea ever! But when the time comes, my introvert feels nervous and wonders who she'll hang out with. That event that seemed like it would be so much fun fills her with dread and she begs to stay in her pajamas and watch Netflix. However, my extrovert feels sad and left out when she hasn't been invited, because she hates not being included—she doesn't want to miss out on *anything*. But, my introvert tells my extrovert that she's glad we weren't invited because she doesn't ever want to leave the house. You get the idea.

What's real and too much and not enough about you, friend?

Noncompliant

(Flipping the Bird at Societal Pressure)

Chapter 23

Au Revoir, Joy-Thief!

"Comparison is the thief of joy!"
THEODORE ROOSEVELT

Whether we're aware or not, we are continually assaulted with images, ideas, standards, and opinions for who we should be. Unrealistic ideals wreak havoc on how we see ourselves as men, women, spiritual anarchists, God-followers, wives, husbands, parents, friends, professionals, homemakers, business owners, interior decorators, pet owners, cooks, and on, and on, and on.

Let's just stop it.

You were imagined by God as a unique creation. Love picked out all your parts. Love named you. There has never been another you, and there will never be another you.

Regretfully, though we may have mountain-top moments of brilliance, most of us feel like we're *not* rocking it at intermittent points in our journeys; that in the competition of life, we are definitely not medaling—not standing on the podium. We may feel like we're *not enough,* or we feel like we're *too much.* Maybe we vacillate between the two.

The voice of *not enough* usually sounds like, "you can't keep up in this race ... you're invisible ... you're drab and uninteresting ... everyone else does it better." Or maybe you feel like you're too much (and I would definitely fit into this category). *Too much* says things like, "you're an offensive, fluorescent lightbulb, overwhelming to the people around you. You're too loud, too opinionated, too passionate ... simmer down!"

Both accusatory voices—feeling not enough or too much—can tempt us to create a flawless facade, perhaps by overcompensating, or, at times, by shrinking. But if you scratch beneath the feigned perfection of any person, even if they're painted shiny and red, underneath you'll see the real stuff: the rust, the dents, the evidence of vandalism. You'll find insecurities, scars, pain. We are all the same. If you've lived at all, you've got the marks to prove it.

Who we are at our core is not random. It's not the luck of the draw. It's not what we have selected. Love made us. Love chose our personalities. Love chose our bodies. Love chose where we would be born, and the families we would be born into. Love knew all our days before any of them came to be.

We are different, unique, custom-made, bespoke. And it's on purpose. A monochromatic and one-dimensional world is not to be desired. So, if we were designed as individuals, why do we continue to compare?

I believe that now, more than ever before, we are set up for comparison, disappointment and discontent. I won't lay *all* of the blame on social media—I happen to love Facebook, Instagram and Pinterest—but I will lay *some* of the blame at its doorstep. There are actual studies that correlate time spent on social media with a lack of contentedness in one's life or a diminishing of self-esteem due to comparison (I'm resisting my academic urge to cite references here, but if you want them, let me know).[1] Social media can easily transport us to a place of longing for things that *aren't* instead of being thankful for the things that *are*.

Spending virtual time in other peoples' lives causes us to live outside our own lives, never being fully present to what is. I regret the many times when I sat playing with my kids, but not really. Though I was physically present, I'd gone somewhere else via the phone in my hand.

When our critical thinking is lulled to sleep, we can forget that much of the content on social media has been curated. We make faulty assumptions about other peoples' lives based on what we see on the surface. We might begin to believe that everyone else fits in and is super connected. Even though we know better—that we're only seeing the best and brightest, the shiny red paint—we unconsciously (or even consciously) compare ourselves. We note that we're not doing it as well; that "their" lives are to be envied.

We see that all the other moms are making healthy, homemade snacks for their kids. We believe the "in love" photos celebrating perfect, idyllic marriages. We see glamorous images of travel, and beautiful homes, and new cars, and successful Harvey Specteresque careers, and perfect children ... and we *know* in our heads it's the highlight reel—that it's the stuff they're (and we're) *choosing* to reveal—but still, it takes a toll. Not one of us is immune. Even the most self-assured and well-adjusted have fallen prey.

As humans, we are never in a static state. We live on a sliding scale—a spectrum—in terms of how we feel about ourselves, how we function, and how we perceive our environments. Diverse seasons bring diverse perceptions and feelings, as well as varying degrees of coping. Where we are on the spectrum can determine whether or not we're a particularly good version of ourselves. The very part of our personality that is a strength when we're walking in wholeness can be a weakness when we're walking in brokenness. It's two sides of the same coin. To clarify, at my best, I'm very efficient and organized. But, at my worst, controlling and frenetic.

When I'm in a good place—feeling content and peaceful (which I very much desire to be), in control (which I very much like to be), when I'm achieving and accomplishing (which I very much love to do), when my kids are getting along, and I've got fresh baking on the counter—I'm less affected by images of perfect, happy children who are kind to one another, of friends going out for dinner together, the family portraits of "normal" unblended family, claims of awesome stay-at-home-mom-ness, homemade everything, and chemical-free cleaning supplies.

But when I'm *not* in such a great place (which can happen to the best of us), those same things can tank me. Even though I *know* you're posting your tidy moments. Even though I know your kids probably fight, too. Even though I know in my heart that you sometimes eat frozen chicken fingers from a box. Even though I know all these things, comparison can creep in. And if I don't stay aware and on top of it, I can start feeling discontented with my life; wishing things were different—all the feelings that do *not* make me the best version of myself.

In this life, we are a combination of nature and nurture—*born this way* and *adaptation* to our circumstances. With nurture, we know that our experiences—that is, what's been done to us, what we've done to others and how things have 'worked out'—definitely allow for the possibility of brokenness and 'less than' versions of ourselves. No one is denying this. But nature would say: *I was meant to be born, chosen, on purpose, and there is goodness for me.*

We are *not* in competition with one another. No one else can steal your life, your calling, your piece of the pie. It's *yours*. Every person has their portion, their path, their life to live. We don't have to arm wrestle for our place in the world. We don't have to urinate in the corners to mark our territory. We don't need to betray and scramble over others to secure our position. We don't need to be stealthy, or sneaky, or the best. We only need to embrace *our* portion and *our* cup. We need only persevere and work hard toward that which is for us.

The tag on my website used to be *Rock Being You*, because my goal in life is to be the *me* that most closely resembles what Love intended. Why? Because it's the best possible, most fulfilled, most content, most effective version of me. When everything around us feels like a measuring stick, or a guideline to which we must adhere, we must grab hold of this truth: we need only be who we were created to be and to offer what we've been given to give.

It's taken a lot of practice and self-control, but I've learned to skirt around the quagmire of comparison. Every now and then, I inadvertently dip a toe, but as those sickening voices of too-much and not-enough announce themselves, I wake up and run reckless in the other direction.

Enjoy social media, but remind yourself to fill in the gaps. Read the unwritten parts of the story. That stay-at-home mom that you're admiring is probably craving some grown-up time. That successful business person that leaves you feeling like a professional failure might be grieving the fact that his, her or their kids spend more time in a daycare than in their real home. Those warm cookies waiting on the counter for kids coming home from school are the only baking that's been done in ages. The happy couple in the photo fought about finances all morning. That luxury cruise used up the last available dollar on their credit card.

I'm not suggesting we view the world through a lens of cynicism and negativity, but to remind us that there is always more than what we see. Don't be fooled by the shiny, red paint.

It's not our job to brighten up or to dim down, but to reflect exactly who we are created to be: brilliant.

So, go ahead. Be brilliant. Bid adieu to the Joy-Thief. It's time to rock being you.

Chapter 24

Hello, My Name Is...

"The beginning of wisdom is to call things by their proper name."
CONFUCIUS

I love naming things. I've even considered that were I to leave teaching for another career, I'd become a professional paint-namer. Or maybe a nailpolish-namer ... because somebody is really doing that! When a paint color is well-named; when the tone and hue are reflected perfectly in the words used to describe, I feel a giant *yes* of agreement in my heart.

It could be argued that, in our house, we've ended up with too many pets, because the mom of the house (that would be me) loves to name things. I do enjoy our animals, but, if I'm honest, choosing pet names might be the best part of getting a new pet for me. I love brainstorming by saying every word out loud that comes to mind; by naming everything I see, and hear, and taste, and smell. I own more baby name books than any person should, especially since the invention of the World Wide Web. Pour me a cup of coffee, put a name book on my lap, and I'll be happy for hours.

Giving names to new humans felt like the ultimate commission. It was a task I accepted with all the gravity and consequence of a royal mandate. Choosing the exact right name for each of my babies was of utmost importance to me. I wanted to like how it sounded, how it looked, what it meant, how it worked with other names. I spent long amounts of time in thoughtful choosing. Until the right name made itself known to me. Of all the possibilities and ideas flying around, one would land and come to roost in my heart. And I would feel the comfortable weight of it. And I would know.

What's your name? We all have earthly names given to us by our people. Maybe your name can be found throughout the generations in your family. Maybe it was trendy and you ended up as one of five Michelles in your first grade classroom. Maybe a sibling was allowed to choose and, as a result, you've spent your whole life explaining how to pronounce or spell your name. My name was assigned because my mother met a woman she admired. I don't believe she gave extensive thought to the actual meaning of my name, but as I became interested in linguistic significance, I learned that Eve Ellen is "life bright."

I happen to like the meaning of my name, and I say yes to it, but whether you like your name or you don't, whether you feel your name holds prophetic promise for you or it doesn't, whether the naming of *you* was carefully crafted or it was a lottery … it doesn't matter. Because Love pondered you intently before you were born. As your physical person was designed, and your personality crafted, Love also named you.

Names are important and knowing who Love says we are is foundational to our identity, both as members of the human race and as individuals. We must memorize the truth, absorb it, and say it out loud. Knowing the truth of our value and identity is the best place to begin, and the best defense against rogue, enemy-namers who would love to see us wrongly labeled.

I don't believe that the divine views us as a collective lump of humans. Love knows us as individuals, uniquely created. As for me, I'm quite certain God thinks I'm hilarious. That may sound heretical to claim that the "divine" thinks I'm funny, but it's true. I'm often aware of laughter when I've been particularly clever. I am conscious of Love's delight in me. I've been named "wild child" and "maverick" (which is essentially an unorthodox or independent-minded person; a free-spirit and a non-conformist. Mmm, pretty much.). Love calls me "unhindered," and says I'm the best version of myself when I live as such.

We need to hear truth above all the rest—above the things broken people have said to us and about us—over the ways we have been faultily named. Maybe there's a name you were called as a child that you've never been able to shake. Maybe a word was used in jest, but it penetrated your heart. Perhaps you have named yourself by believing your own corrupt inner monologue.

Very often, we believe what is being reflected back to us by broken vessels. I am better able to understand this idea using the analogy of a broken mirror. While the glass may remain intact within the frame of the mirror, it is shattered and fragmented. I can recognize myself enough within the reflected image to know it is me, but the image is distorted and broken. This is often what happens when we listen to these shattered, fragmented voices. There is enough truth in what's being said to tempt us to believe it, but it's not a full and clear picture of who we are; it's broken. So how do we discern the truth of who we are?

Changing our names is definitely not as easy as right-clicking for a drop-down menu that gives us the option to rename. But it can be done. When the faulty names get spoken, whether by others or by ourselves, it's time to fact check for truth. We need to learn to hear the voice of Love above all others.

We can rename things by simply repeating the new name over and over. When I had children, I became intrigued with the language learning process. After months of labeling and naming everything in their environments, my babies would begin to point and name using the correct words. I also witness this dynamic as a French teacher. If I were truly dark and twisty, I'd undertake an experiment that would really screw up my students; I'd teach the incorrect names for things. And then, by continuing to use the incorrect words, the names would stick. How about, "that's not a dog, it's an apple (Ce n'est pas un chien, c'est une pomme)."

This may seem a ridiculous example, but it actually happens in real life. We use the wrong names for ourselves all the time: "I'm stupid, lazy, harsh. I'm ugly. I'm a terrible mom." When we repeat these names over and over, they stick. So, call yourself by your *true* names, by your *real* names.

Say them out loud. Say them until you absorb them. Say them until you believe them.

I am firmly in the camp of Maya Angelou who said, "Words are things. You must be careful, careful about calling people out of their names, using racial pejoratives, and sexual pejoratives, and all that ignorance. Don't do that. Someday we'll be able to measure the power of words. I think they are things. They get on the walls. They get in your wallpaper. They get in your rugs, in your upholstery, and your clothes, and finally into you."[1]

I may not know you personally, but I can promise you your name is not "Failure." "Bitchy" or "Weak" or "Insecure" were never selected as the defining tags for you. If the names you are hearing do not line up with the truth of Love, then they are not true. It's time to re-name. Sit quietly and ask Love for your true name. Stay there and listen— and when you start to perceive names soaked in loving kindness, don't reject them. Don't disqualify by saying, "Oh, those are just my own thoughts." Write them down. If others share loving words with you, write them down. Compile a list of the names and descriptors chosen for you.

In this world, we will be mis-identified, labeled, and inaccurately named, so we must speak truthfully to ourselves, and answer only to our true names.

Chapter 25

You Are Not the Only One

"There's a place where we don't have to be alone. Every time that you call out, you're a little less alone. If you only say the word, from across the silence, your voice is heard."

DEAR EVAN HANSEN

When we're struggling in a hard season, or we seem to have misplaced the best version of ourselves, it can feel isolated and lonely. Even though our healthy selves know better, our unhealthy selves absorb filtered images and carefully curated posts on social media, falling prey to the lie that we're the only ones feeling this way.

An 'alone' scenario that frequently plays out for me, (and that I should likely leave unspoken, lest I reveal what a total sci-fi weirdo I really am), is that I'm the only person left alive on the face of the planet. This bizarre thought usually visits me at the crack of dawn, as I am almost always the first one awake in my household. When it's quiet and dark and still, I can be tempted to believe that the apocalypse has happened and I've clearly been left behind. I'm always relieved when I see another living creature, even if it's my cat. Thank you, Stella, for scratching at the door … and for not being a zombie.

Wild, dystopian imaginings aside, there are many scenarios in life that leave us feeling like the only one.

The only ones who are dissatisfied.

The only ones not nailing the parenting gig.

The only ones who don't have a group of intimate, life-long friends.

The only ones who can't afford groceries, let alone luxurious vacations.

The only ones experiencing a desert season.

The only ones suffering with chronic pain or illness.

The only ones whose kids argue with them and talk back constantly.

The only ones shedding tears over a kitchen that needs to be cleaned *again*.

The only ones feeling like there *must* be more than this.

The only ones who weren't invited.

The only ones feeling unseen.

The only ones grieving what life *used* to look like.

The only ones with anxiety.

The only ones putting high-fructose corn syrup treats in the kids' lunches.

The only ones feeling stuck and unmotivated.

The only ones asking if God still sees us.

The only ones avoiding seven baskets of unfolded, wrinkled laundry.

The only ones who shrieked "*Get. In. The. Car.*" at our kids this morning.

The only ones marvelling that life is simultaneously too big *and* too small for us.

No matter your experience, I promise you, *you are not the only one.*

While I believe God's intention is for us to live interconnected, the world would *love* for us to believe that we are alone. Whether by using shame to keep us quiet and skillfully disguising our weakness *OR* by using self-pity to lure us into the belief that no one can possibly understand *our* lot in life...the result is the same. Isolation. Feeling like the only one.

The only way to bust out of solitary confinement is to be honest and real. We need to drag our stuff into the light so that we (and others) can see it all for what it is: a shared, human experience, not unique to us, not insurmountable. Courage and authenticity help to unlock the doors of our prisons.

Sometimes we fear revealing our true selves because of past experiences. Maybe when you risked honesty, your story was diminished, or one-upped, or you were told to *"Get over it!"* (I don't know about you, but someone telling me to get over it has *never* helped me to get over it. Pro tip: These words are *rarely* helpful). Or maybe your vulnerability was met with blank stares and undisguised judgement.

Sometimes the prison bars aren't even installed by others; we do it ourselves. We tell ourselves we're selfish and self-absorbed for feeling what we feel. We measure our hard things against the extreme plight of others, hesitant to share because we know there are far worse things in the world than our own personal struggle.

I'm certainly not advocating negativity, but rather honesty. Honesty does not equal complaint. Speaking vulnerably about hard things does not mean you're a whiner. And truly, resolving to stoically endure doesn't really serve us well. In fact, it tends to perpetuate feelings of loneliness and isolation.

But feelings are *not* the boss of us! We can push back against fear, shame, and self-pity by intentionally disassembling the facade that we so carefully constructed. Though we *meant* for it to protect us, it *actually* separated us. It separated us from who we were created to be, and, thus, from others.

When we share our true selves, it gives others permission to do the same.

No one has it all together, even those in carefully groomed packages. And on the flip side, very few who self-identify as "train wrecks" actually qualify for the label either. There is so much pressure to look like we're doing it well … to pretend we've *so* got this. But it's impossible. It's fake. And if we don't want to feel like fakers, we need to stop faking. If we don't want to feel like the only one, we need to stop acting like the only one.

But what if I cast my pearls before swine? But what if they cannot be trusted? But what if they no longer like me?

You can trust *you,* and you can trust Love to give you discernment. You'll quickly realize who can't handle authenticity and who can. Who can't reciprocate and who can. The ones who *can* are worth their weight in gold. Hold on to these people. And determine to *be* one of these people.

We have to push back against the evil lie that we're alone. We have to be willing to go first with our stories. We have to share our true selves. We have to be honest about the amazing parts *and* the hard parts. We have to offer our joys *and* our worries. When we risk the words *"I feel like the only one who … "* more often than not, we'll be met with nods of understanding and sighs of relief.

Let's ask Love, who dreamed us up, and formed us, and delights in us, to unlock our prison doors. And then, let's help others to open theirs. Be willing to go first. Be willing to listen with empathy. Create sacred space by saying, *"Yeah, me too."* We are *not* alone. We are *not* the only ones.

Chapter 26

Your Part Matters

---

*"The world needs dreamers and the world needs doers, but
most of all the world needs dreamers who do."*
SARAH BAN BREATHNACH

When it comes to making space for creativity, underneath all
of our valid reasons and excuses lie the deeper questions: Is
what I'm doing good enough? Does it even matter? Am I making a
difference?

Writing has felt complicated for me this summer. As the school
year ended, so ended a schedule that housed defined times and built-
in spaces dedicated to creating. Though I've been a closet writer my
entire adult life with no particular pattern or schedule, I quickly
became accustomed to having a designated day. And, honestly? That
one day a week made me feel legitimate...like a "real" writer.

All year long, I could jot down thoughts that were percolating,
confident that I'd have time to give them voice when my *writing
day* came. It's been difficult to find time because, though I'm off for
the summer as a teacher, so are my children. Because the schedule is
less structured, so am I. (I swear I get more done when I'm working

full-time!) Ideas flood my brain as I make meals, clean up, drive here, there, and everywhere. But I can't seem to get to them.

Defined writing times are no more. The summer routine is unpredictable, and I'll be back to work full-time before I know it. This altered rhythm has thrown me off and I've been struggling to regain my footing. Though I know it's not the truth, it has felt like losing ground, like skidding backwards down the mountain I worked so earnestly to summit.

In times of creative frustration, we could point our fingers to a lack of routine. We could indict our busy lives and work schedules. We could hang it on a lack of inspiration. For me, I could easily blame my inner paralysis on a lack of alone time (which I *really* need) in which to formulate and work out my ideas. But I actually think there is more to it. And I don't think I'm alone in this.

As humans, we need to feel like our part matters, that what we're doing is meaningful, that we're actually contributing in a way that makes a difference. Whenever I question whether my offering has value or I doubt my ability or I compare myself to others, my creativity becomes paralyzed.

Is what I'm doing good enough? Does it even matter? Am I making a difference?

The answer is *yes*.

We need to know in our knower that our value isn't dependent on what we do or create or produce. Our value is not dependent on fame nor recognition. Our value is innate as humans. We will never be more loved or accepted than we already are, at our worst or at our best. And what we create has value in and of itself, without being recognized or celebrated or rewarded. Art for art's sake is a good enough reason.

On a road trip during this time, my companion listened to me wrestle through all of the angsty thoughts I'd been entertaining. You should actually feel *very* sorry for them because I was in one heck of a self-analyzing, ruminating, melancholy kind of space. It sounded a bit like this:

"What. Am. I. Doing? Why am I even writing? Is anyone even reading it? Do I even want them to read it? Maybe it's total crap! *Gasp* Maybe I'm humiliating myself and don't even realize it?! I feel deeply that I have to keep writing ... I *have* to do this, I *want* to do this ... but *all* of the people in the whole entire world are already writing. There are one billion writers and bloggers sending their stuff into the world. There are so many ideas and words and stories. The world is *saturated*. What could I possibly add?"

Not my finest moment, as you can see. And my companion (who had worked in the music industry alongside musicians and creative people forever) said, "Umm, Elle? You sound like every artist, musician, writer and creative person since the beginning of time. You're normal. What you're feeling is not unique. What you're doing *does* matter."

When I snapped out of my funk and paid attention to my stream of consciousness, I was annoyed that I'd been duped into giving air space to this destructive line of thinking. Welcome to being human.

What excuses are keeping you from doing that thing you *long* to do? What thought processes are undermining your confidence? What's making you believe that what you have to offer isn't worthy?

Since I began writing intentionally, my bottom-line purpose has been obedience. I felt a divine invitation into this, and I said yes. The value has been in taking a risk, moving beyond what is comfortable. If my musings help a reader in some small way to feel inspired, or understood, or not alone, that's even *more* than enough. I need to return my gaze to what I'm called to and resist measuring myself against what others are doing. I need to stay in my own lane.

We can become stifled, feeling small and insignificant, when we believe that our gift doesn't matter or that it doesn't measure up. It's a lie! There is room for all of us … and for all of our creations. Scarcity mentality says there's only one pie and we have to fight to get our piece. Abundance says, there's enough. Eat as much pie as you want! Look at how many songs are written using the same seven notes and how many books are written using the same thirty thousand-ish words.

God's book describes us as being parts of the body. Though we might be tempted to esteem certain body parts higher than others, especially those that are highly visible, like eyes and hair and hands, the reality is that the unseen parts are *as* or *more* important. Though hair adds beauty, without internal organs, we die. All of the parts belong, different but functioning together. All of the parts are necessary and valuable and beautiful.

If you don't show up, the world misses out on something original. If you don't play your part, the song won't be the same. We need all of the colors and thoughts and sounds and words and movements to make the world bright and rich and beautiful.

Creativity has many expressions. What's your thing? Is it an act of service for one person, building a website, fostering a positive classroom environment, writing a song, loving the people right in front of you, photography, being vocal on an issue, learning to bake, speaking to thousands of listeners, sculpting something new, living with integrity even when no one is looking, knitting, athleticism, learning another language, painting, preparing food for your family, letting your thoughts flow onto a page? Don't hold back. Your part matters.

So often as humans, we'd rather run before we crawl. We want to begin as experts. We want to be the best. We don't want to risk failure or embarrassment or mediocrity. We don't want to start at the beginning, so we don't start.

But what if success doesn't mean being the best? What if the truest sign of success is that we determine to humbly play our part—that we risk putting ourselves out there and we keep going? What if being remarkable means that we keep our candle lit and that we vehemently refuse to be snuffed out?

The metric for success doesn't need to be how many likes we get on Facebook, or how many followers we have on Twitter, or whether or not we have a gallery showing, or a publishing deal, or a record label. Sure, we might want these concrete assurances of success, but at a more foundational level, the *win* is that you are doing that thing you were made to do. We have to trust that in our saying *yes*—in our being willing, in our perseverance, in our determination to carve out the time—things will unfold as they were intended.

I'm not a fatalist. I believe there are individual plans for each of us, but I also believe that we have free will to choose. Though certainly, dreams *can* be delivered on silver platters, more often, we need to engage our God-given wills and get off our butts. However, in the same breath, I'd argue that neither do we need to hustle and strive to realize our dreams. It's always both: the difficult tension of trusting totally *and* working hard, holding things loosely *and* contending for the fulfillment of the promise.

One of the biggest impediments to creativity is waiting until we have time. Very often, we want to wait for things to fall into place before we begin. But the "right" time won't come; it's an elusive, dangling carrot. To be *more* than dreamers, we need to start painting, start singing, start cooking, start writing, start reaching out, start connecting. Just start. Sometimes starting is the hardest part.

Risk doing that thing you were made for. Pursue your dream, attain that goal, create something for no other reason than it's beautiful and you *can't not*. Make the time, even when there isn't time. Push through your insecurities because we need that burning thing inside of you. Whether it's a flickering pilot light or a roaring fire, it is enough to diminish gloom in our world.

And now, back to my summer funk and the end of this story. While talking with my sister about the struggle it's been to write this summer and how it's felt like I'm skidding backwards down the mountain, my then 11-year-old daughter piped up from the couch beside me:

"So, run back up the mountain, Mom!"

Mic drop. Out of the mouths of babes. Her simple exhortation to *keep going* punched me right in the gut. So, I'm applying my sweet girl's sage advice. I will keep creating. I will continue to give voice to the ideas that swirl and build and all but explode in my brain.

I am running back up the mountain. Wanna come?

Chapter 27

Fully You

*"To be nobody but yourself in a world that's doing its best
to make you somebody else, is to fight the hardest fight
you are ever going to fight. Never stop fighting."*

E.E. CUMMINGS

Y ou are the only *you* that has ever existed and who will *ever* exist.
Your job is to be you in all of your weirdness, and awesomeness,
and weakness, and brilliance. It should be easy, right? It should be the
default. Being yourself should be what you do best, what happens
naturally. To maneuver and manipulate who you are into the mold
offered by society should be the hard work. Why is it, so often, the
reverse?

Whether we acknowledge it or not, we humans have a deep need
to be known. And in order to be known, we must be honest about
how we feel. We have to name our likes and dislikes, our hopes and
fears. If we hide who we really are, we will never truly feel known.

You being fully you means, not only being honest with others
about who you are, but also with yourself. It means paying attention
so that you recognize your own strengths and weaknesses, things that
happen naturally, and areas where you need work. Your passions—the

things that move you, that break your heart, that get you all fired up—these are all clues to who you were made to be. These are in you on purpose.

In his song "Ahead by a Century," Gord Downey sings, *"no dress rehearsal, this is our life."[1]* This is our *one* life. We can't figure it out during the rehearsal, work out the kinks, and then bring it. This is it.

As an educator, I allocate an immense amount of discussion time toward self-concept. As these poor unsuspecting darlings navigate the tumultuous adolescent years, I want them to be overfilled with self-esteem and self-love. I validate who they are, cheering for them to be just that, saying, "If you love chess, *love* chess! If you love fluorescent orange, wear fluorescent orange! Like what you like...you do you!" I want to send them off confident in who they are because society is going to push against them and tempt them to conform.

While I don't strive for people to like me, because I'm human, occasionally, I wrestle when they don't. The temptation can be to falsify or become beige so others will approve, but that always backfires. If I'm fully myself and people like me, then I'll know they really like *me*. Posturing is exhausting, and wreaks havoc on self-awareness, separating us from our true selves.

I have zero interest in faking it. I don't like it in myself, and I don't like it in other people. I crave authenticity. Though it can be complicated and messy, almost guaranteeing we'll see one another's worst parts up close, it's the only means by which we can truly connect. Removed and distant, we may not discern the scars and chin hairs, but we also miss out on truly knowing and being known. Up close, we see the broken and the beautiful, the visceral and the real.

In my late teens, I felt a divine invitation to embrace maverickdom: to be real and to push back against conformity. I was invited to live honestly so that others could, too. At the time, it wasn't a mandate I perceived to be overly spiritual or weighty, but a couple of decades later, I now grasp how holy it is to be who we truly are.

While living freely and truthfully sounds idyllic, it's not without its trouble. Because, as it turns out, not everyone wants you to be real. They, whoever "they" are, might not like it.

When you're honest about the hard things, they might utter statements like, "*you're negative*" or "*stop complaining*." Or they'll be aghast and judgy that you live without shame of your past (because apparently they don't understand that you can *really* be forgiven and live without shame). They might take offense that you *actually* like yourself (accusing you of believing yourself to be *so special* and *all that*). Sometimes they'll be upset by your freedom and speak resentful statements like, "*It must be nice to be so free.*" Almost as though they think you got lucky.

What they don't understand is that it's not a personality trait, but a minute by minute choice. And often, it's terribly hard work. And more often than that, it's an all out inner street fight.

Some of my worst wounds have come from very nice people who, in their humanity, have been threatened by me being me. People who have made assumptions about who I am based on the snapshots they could see. I don't fault them because, regretfully, I know I've doled out my fair share of unsolicited judgement, as well.

It's easy to tell one another to ignore what people say, to shake it off. But combatting hurtful accusations is brutally hard work. I regularly affirm to my own children and my students that if someone doesn't like you, it doesn't mean there is anything wrong with you. You don't have to be everyone's cup of tea. Though I believe this with all my heart, it doesn't mean we won't feel the sting of rejection. Feel it, own what needs to be owned, speak the truth to yourself, and let it go.

Here's the thing, one person liking themselves is not an indictment on the other with the purpose of making them feel *less than*.

Me actually liking myself should not make you feel diminished. If anything, it should give you permission to like *yourself*! I think I'm awesome ... and guess what? I think you're awesome, too! We are not in competition.

In her book *A Return to Love*, Marianne Williamson writes:

> *"Our deepest fear is not that we are inadequate. Our deepest fear is that we are powerful beyond measure. It is our light, not our darkness that most frightens us. We ask ourselves, who am I to be brilliant, gorgeous, talented, fabulous? Actually, who are you not to be? You are a child of God. Your playing small does not serve the world. There is nothing enlightened about shrinking so that other people won't feel insecure around you. We are all meant to shine, as children do. We were born to make manifest the glory of God that is within us. It's not just in some of us; it's in everyone. And as we let our own light shine, we unconsciously give other people permission to do the same. As we are liberated from our own fear, our presence automatically liberates others."[2]*

Being fully you requires intentionality and determination. But, there's no right or wrong way to do you, no measuring stick. There are no laws, only grace. The trouble is that a lot of us still live like there's a checklist, making sure that we *do* and *don't do*. We adhere to some rituals, while avoiding others. Say this, don't say that, act like this, don't be seen there. Barf. Yes, sometimes it would likely be easier to know that if I do certain things and avoid others, I can be assured I'm on the right path, but it's a losing gamble. You will never achieve the law's demands or satisfy its requirements.

Being fully you requires wisdom and maturity. It is not an excuse to stop caring for or respecting the feelings and opinions of others. It's not permission to hurt or offend people with the cop out "I'm just being me" or "this is how God made me!" There's no excuse for mean, intentionally hurtful behavior. Above all else, love.

Being fully you requires discernment. Authenticity does not ask you to be indiscriminate, throwing your precious pearls to swine. I had to learn this one the hard way. In other words, know your audience. Not every person needs to hear the details, and certainly not everyone has earned the right to hold your story. Choose your people carefully. Not fearfully, but carefully.

Brené Brown presented a TedTalk a number of years ago entitled, "The Power of Vulnerability."[3] After discovering it, I watched it no less than twenty times, and also made everyone I know watch it. She talks about the power and necessity of vulnerability. In her research, she has learned that vulnerability is the birthplace of connection and creativity. If we want authentic relationships, and if we want to be known, we have to risk. We have to be vulnerable.

When we pretend to have it all together or "present" as perfect, it renders us inaccessible to others, perceived as a threat, or sniffed out as a fake. In either scenario, we end up alienated and not connected. When we are real, it diffuses competition. We can connect because we're sharing the story and fighting the same fight.

The benefits of being fully you are not just for you. Beyond the joy of feeling known, being true to who you are creates a pathway for others to follow. When we are real, others can be real. When we are brave, others can be brave. When we are honest, others will feel safe enough to be honest.

Somebody has to go first. Be the one.

Let's decide to be the kind of people that allow others to breathe a sigh of relief. No more perpetuating the lie that we have it all together. Let's tell the truth so that others can tell the truth. Let's be vulnerable so that we can know others and be known by them. Let's honor who we were created to be.

Here's to keeping it real, friends.

Chapter 28

Sometimes Rescue Looks Like Failure

"No tree, it is said, can grow to heaven unless
its roots reach down to hell."

CARL G. JUNG

Someone once told me a story that often resurfaces in my thoughts when I find myself longing for a shortcut. In the midst of a hard season, he asked some friends to pray with him. After some well-intentioned prayers, pleading with God for rescue, one wise and seasoned man spoke. With tears streaming down his face he said, "You need to travel your road. And don't let anyone pull you out too early or you'll miss what God has for you." And that's it, precisely.

What I want is peace. What I want is success. What I want is to have more than enough. What I want is an absence of conflict. What I want is to win. What I want is for everything to be easy. What I want is for people to like me. What I want is lots of candy. What I want is for someone else to do this hard thing. What I want is to be plucked out of this wearisome situation.

But what I *want* doesn't necessarily get me to a place I want to be.

I've come to understand that easy doesn't mean right, just as hard doesn't mean wrong. These organizing thought structures have failed us. We put *struggle* in the bad column and *plenty* in the good column when, frequently, it's plenty that's bad for us and struggle that is good for us. Sometimes a miracle *does* airlift us right out of situations, but more often, the process of rescue looks like hard work or limbo or failure. We are allowed, even *invited*, to walk difficult and dangerous pathways. Because Love sees how it will benefit us and knows the end goal, even when we cannot.

Sometimes rescue is hard. *Sometimes it even looks like failure.*

God said these words to me during a particularly difficult season. A season I was railing against. A season where I could not determine if the pressure had its origin in goodness or in trouble. A season where I couldn't sense whether I was to embrace and grow *or* grit my teeth and fight. I only knew I wanted out, or, at the very least, wanted to be looking back on it from the other side. But when I heard the words, I understood. What had felt like death would actually produce life, if I would allow it.

From my human perspective and limited understanding, my experience during this phase of life felt like failure, like shrinking. I was a leader who had stepped back from leading. I was a capable person who no longer felt capable. I went from being the one who could handle it, to no longer handling it. I went from being a known participant, to being an unknown bystander. It felt hard and embarrassing and weak. And I do not like to be weak.

Weak and irresponsible are, to me, the most cutting of insults. My innate response in any situation is to take care of it. My first-born, overdeveloped sense of responsibility kicks into gear with a "don't worry, I've got this" arrogance. But not this time. I was at a loss.

Once, I had been a mature tree with expansive branches, fully in leaf, but it seemed I was no longer so. More than just the shedding of leaves during an autumn season, it felt as though I had been cut down to the ground. Branches and foliage gone. Nothing living. Only a stump remaining.

The internal vacillating during this phase was intense, enough to give me emotional and spiritual whiplash. I wondered, constantly, "Is this divine or is this evil?" "Is this good or is this bad?" In the end, I actively chose to disregard binaries. I decided to accept what was instead of planning my escape or orchestrating my own rescue. Even if enemies *did* mean it for my destruction, Love could use it for my good.

Though I knew this pruning practice to be true in my own garden—that to strengthen root systems, we must cut back the part above ground—in my own life, it was painful and counter-intuitive. To the natural eye, things were falling apart, but from Love's perspective, great gains were being made.

Trusting God, I embraced my stump-dom. And then one day, I heard a whisper: *"You let me cut you down and now your roots are strong and glorious."* In my mind's eye, I saw myself, again, as the pitiful stump. But this time, instead of seeing only brokenness, I gazed deeper and saw my own elaborate root systems. My roots were beautiful, like the inverse reflection of a tree. In a moment of epiphany, I understood that these roots were a foreshadowing of what I would, again, become. That in order to become more fully who I was created to be, my roots had to be able to support and balance the growth.

I won't glorify the struggle or pretend that I loved the discomfort of that season (or *any* of the stressful seasons that have come before and will, inevitably, come again). I didn't always weather it gracefully; in fact, I gritted my teeth and endured most every second of it. But it was worth it.

And now, on closer inspection, I see that little green shoots have unfurled from the humble stump—new growth that I believe, in faith, will mirror the strong, far-reaching roots.

It wasn't failure after all. It was rescue.

Chapter 29

Speak Up

"Speak the truth, even if your voice shakes."

MAGGIE KUHN

How very apt that my Facebook post from years ago should resurface in my 'memories' this morning, perhaps as a harbinger to say the thing that must be said. Though I am Canadian, this American event impacted me greatly.

Parents, teachers, leaders:

This is the part where we move from subtle, child-directed conversations on kindness, justice, and compassion to intentional, focused instruction on what it looks like to stand up, to have courage, to live with integrity. #notgoingwiththeflow

#raisingupadifferentgeneration

#makinggoodunderpressure

#actjustlylovemercywalkhumbly

(November 9, 2016)

I am not a debater. Though I hold strong beliefs and do not mince words when called upon, you will never find me on a soap box in

Hyde Park. Nor will you find me *entertained* by the person on the soapbox, holding court in Speakers' Corner. I do not enjoy debate, where one party attempts, by any means, to convince the other of his, her or their perceived correct thought. No thank you. Being talked *at* is a massive turn off for me.

What I love is honest conversation. Thoughtful dialog. A balance of listening and speaking.

Because of my abhorrence for hot-headed debate, my tendency has been to physically leave the space or to go radio silent when people begin expostulating on their latest issues-based rhetoric. While I'll talk easily about my thoughts and interpretations in secure spaces and in the context of relationship, I've found it easier to fly under the radar on certain inflammatory topics.

(Side note: If you know me personally, you're probably thinking "Sheesh, that was you mincing words?!" Ha. Yup. There's a lot more in there than I let out, friends. I would terrify you if I said all. of. the. things.)

I'm not saying that I *don't* speak up. Because I definitely do. Just not in an argumentative, platformy, "I *will* convince you" manner. It's more in a *sharing my heart* kind of way.

Though people perceive me to be honest, which I am, it's arguably *as* true that I've often played the role of "maverick." I can belong in a space without necessarily adhering to every tenet held by the larger group. In my heart, I can say, "Yes to that, yes to that ... and *no way* to that." Typically, I've been able to preserve my integrity while holding in tension the parts with which I don't agree.

But at what point is it no longer okay to be quiet? When do we drift over the line from *quietly respectful* to *bystander*?

I am a teacher. I spend most of my days with young people. So the words *bully, victim,* and *bystander* are common vernacular for me.

Only one of those three roles is innocent. When we stand back and withhold our opinion, saying, "*this doesn't affect me*" or "*this is none of my business*," we align ourselves with the bully. If we don't speak up on behalf of the victim, we are, by default, supporting the antagonist.

This word, bystander, has become more and more of a thorn in my side of late. It's become uncomfortable. It's become personal. Because I've realized that, in omission—staying silent, opting out, carefully controlling my tongue—I've been contributing to the problem.

Sometimes maturity is being quiet. Sometimes maturity is speaking up.

Taking a stand requires a level of courage that most of us don't feel we embody. We are highly aware that it will cost us something. But the beautiful thing about courage is that it doesn't mean we are fearless. It means we acknowledge the fear and proceed regardless.

In my family, I've taught my children to respectfully advocate for themselves when necessary and to watch for those who need their help. No, they are not perfect kids. They are passionate and opinionated and spazzy. (*It's the strangest thing—I honestly cannot imagine where these traits came from!*). They are real, mostly kind, but sometimes unkind, breathtaking, imperfect humans. And over and over, I have been immensely proud when they have extended kindness to fringe people and have stuck up for those who weren't able to advocate for themselves.

The part we sometimes forget, however, is that doing this—using our voices for others, sticking up for people, speaking truth—will usually cost us something. My kids have learned the hard way that if you tell a bunch of boys in your Phys. Ed. class to stop calling another female student "*whale*," they will likely turn that venom toward you and you'll now be teased incessantly. Or if you call out the ones who have renamed a bigger boy in an orange t-shirt "*pumpkin*," they'll turn that rage toward you and make your life hell. It's so hard, but it's still the right thing.

Interspersed amidst the past couple of years, I've experienced themes during times of prayer, in conversation, and within my own intensive thought life that, until recently, I didn't recognize were linked. It's always interesting when we turn around and suddenly see how we were being prepared for something, how those seemingly unrelated events and experiences were actually weaving a storyline that now makes sense.

In this current season of realization, I've been very aware of what speaking up will cost me. I've been weighing it all out. I've been moving slowly toward what I believe is right, all the while asking that the cup be taken from me. I will *always* be willing to walk where integrity is leading, but I've had some definite sadness about parts of it. I'm certain it's the next right thing, but it's not without loss.

On one particular morning, as I wrestled again with the positives and negatives of where I am in contrast to where I feel I'm being called, I was reminded clearly that Love doesn't do bad trades. It's just the opposite. *Oh yeah, God. I forgot that you give beauty for ashes, joy for mourning and a spirit of praise for despair.*

Here's what I am now remembering and relearning: if we are feeling called to action. If we are feeling the weight of a conversation that needs to be had. If we have fire in our bones and can't *not* say the thing. If something has been cornering us and it's time to push back. Whatever it is. If God is leading us to do the next right thing, it might not be without consequence, but we can be sure it will be worth it.

> *"All that is necessary for the triumph of evil is that good men [and women] do nothing."*[1] *(Edmund Burke)*

Chapter 30

To Drink or To Dump

"You must not lose faith in humanity. Humanity is an ocean; if a few drops of the ocean are dirty, the ocean does not become dirty."
MAHATMA GANDHI

I've been disgusted with humanity in the last year or two—with individuals, with groups, with organizations. There have been some major collisions that have caused me to experience *soul concussions*, and then many other bumps in varying degrees of severity that, as with a concussion, have actually been more dangerous than the original blow.

I don't like it. I don't enjoy this way of thinking. Or feeling. I'm sad and disheartened and angry. This cynicism and despise is not me. I don't want it. It's so bad that I've even Googled: *"How do I recover from a loss of faith in humanity?"* It's also bad enough that I've checked myself into 'wellness rehab' for a few days. I need to figure some things out. I need to be with my thoughts. I need to write, and pray, and sleep, and recover. Because one more *soul blow* in my current state could cause permanent damage.

And so, I'm alone at the lake. Hours in, I already see more clearly. *"Let it go"* is written on a coffee cup sitting on the counter. It contains the image of a balloon, and not Elsa's face, but this does nothing to deter the earworm that has now taken hold. Regardless, it feels like a deeply spiritual invitation.

Let it go. Let *what* go?

My high idealism? My disgust? My anger? My disappointment? My hope? My dreams of kingdom come? My barely existent, and possibly ludicrous, belief that people are mostly good?

What do I *need* to let go of? To be happy. To be content. To have peace. To find solace. To be free. *For. The. Love!*

And if I let *it* go, does it then mean that the bad guys win? That I am wishy-washy? Lukewarm? That I've ceased caring? Stopped holding the line? That I've forfeited my integrity?

Occasionally in the past, I've been known to apply the failures of the *one* to the *whole*, as in, this man failed me … all men will fail me. This girl is mean … all girls are mean. This situation sucks … my whole life sucks.

This manner of thinking is not balanced, true, or healthy.

But the reverse, using the *whole* to characterize the *one*, is also problematic. And that's where I've been lately. Humanity, on the whole, *IS* largely selfish, evil, flawed, broken, corrupt.

And I've allowed my feelings about humanity to affect my feelings about humans.

But when I come in close—when I focus on the one—I see individual beauty and goodness. Individuals who are trying to live with integrity in a broken system that doesn't allow for integrity. Individuals who show up with flowers, even when they feel flowers are not enough, because they don't know what else to do, but they want to do *something*. Individuals who send you a text or buy you a drink to remind you that they esteem you and love you. Individuals who, though perhaps not strong enough to fight off the danger on their own, come close to you, and gather 'round, like a herd of elephants protecting their new mamas and babies, their weak, and their vulnerable.

I've often explained to my children, and to my students, that if you look for the hard stuff, you'll find it. And if you look for the good stuff, you'll find it. It's a matter of where we lay our gaze. So right now, I'm working *so* hard to look closely at this good stuff. And these small moments, examined carefully under a magnifying glass, are what is healing me.

My temptation when things feel unjust or wrong is to hold my ground. I'd rather be alone than bend my values. But perhaps that high idealism is better fodder for movies, or poetry, or the dream of youth. It was a successful posture for the first half of my life, but now, it doesn't seem viable. It no longer seems to be where health, safety, and wholeness abide. Maybe, as with most things, there are no binaries to be found here.

My idealism and my beliefs about what is Right (yes, capital R) have always been strengths of my character and have guided my decisions. But what if, in the extreme, these qualities allow me to see only the drops that are dirty in a vast ocean that is not? Do I abandon what is mostly good because of the elements that are not?

Or do I invite my idealism to descend from its high horse, temper its rigid stance, and walk among the real-life broken things; to look into the eyes of so many individuals who are trying their best, doing what they can, and standing quietly in support, even if they cannot raise their voices.

However, context does matter. In a restaurant—where I am not necessarily connected to the people around me in an intimate way, and the storyline is a single thread—a fly in my wine, or lipstick on my glass (that isn't mine) are grounds for complaint … and a new glass of wine, please. I'd rather not drink from the dirty glass of a stranger. But when I'm in the home of someone I know, someone with whom I share a connection and where there are many stories in addition to this one thread, I'd likely dump the wine into another glass (that I get from the cupboard myself), or wipe the lipstick off with my sleeve and keep on going. In my own home, I've fished many a fruit fly out of my wine and then continued to enjoy the wine. If it's good wine, I'm not wasting it.

Let's extend this to real life. If there's no connection in a particular context—whether work, or church, or a relationship—then lipstick on your glass can cause repulsion and disgust. Dump it out. New glass, please. But if there is intimacy, and the wine is really good, then remove the damn fly. Keep drinking. Keep enjoying.

There is so much that is hard right now: pandemic, infidelity, injustice, hatred, financial strain, illness, corruption, evil. All of these horrific things really do exist. And they really do influence our experience. *But* we can live as mavericks in the midst of these things. We may have no choice but to live in the Matrix, but we can be those who actively subvert it—by giving flowers, by offering forgiveness, by standing alongside. We mavericks are those who can exist within a broken system without necessarily (while definitely *not*) adhering to all, or even any, of its tenets.

We must all decide what is worth it, and what isn't. It isn't about sacrificing our integrity. It's about choosing what we can and cannot live with.

Maybe it's a great glass of wine, but in present company, it tastes like vinegar. Maybe it's great wine in a dirty glass, but the connection is intimate, so you choose to enjoy it anyway. Drink it or dump it. There isn't a wrong answer here. You don't have to drink the wine. And you don't have to *not* drink the wine. And you certainly don't have to pour out the whole bottle because your lofty (and perhaps, romantic and unreasonable) ideals tell you you should *(ahem ... Ellen!)*.

In this season, I must look for goodness—the individual kindnesses, the small acts, the quiet conversations, and even the unsuccessful measures performed with good intentions—and allow *these* to flavor my perception of humanity. Not the few drops that are dirty.

I've decided to remove the fly and keep drinking because I like the people I'm with. And it's really great wine.

Chapter 31

Keeping It Real III

I don't really *do* scary movies. It's not only the jump scares and gratuitous gore that repel me—it's that my imagination works *very* well on its own. I already have to avoid looking at the dead body that is *probably* in my bathtub when I get up to use the bathroom each night. My creativity needs no help, so as much as possible, I try to avoid adding additional content to the outrageous ideas that already live in my brain.

✳

I am an achiever. Efficiency and effectiveness are my personal guideposts. Lists are my favorite. I feel ridiculously overjoyed when I accomplish tasks. A job 99% finished is *not* finished to me. Only 100% gets checked off the list. I am competitive, not with others but with myself. My brain automatically schedules me, even when there is nothing official to be done. For example, first coffee, then journaling, then a walk. And none of this stresses me out. Quite the contrary...I feel fulfilled.

✳

I write a lot of "hot letters." Not the sexy kind, but the kind Abraham Lincoln used to write. When Abe was angry with someone, he would compose what he dubbed a "hot letter." Instead of sending it immediately to the recipient, he would set it aside to be read later with a cool head. Many of his letters were later found unsigned and unsent. Wise man, that Abe.

I use this practice in my own daily life. *Everything* goes into my journal. But it can never be read by you or anyone because lots of what is inside is fury and process. I am a person who feels things deeply, so it is important for me to barf onto the page and say everything I need to say ... but doing so to a person's face, sending an email, or posting online while upset or furious is always a bad idea. While we want to be honest about our hurt when warranted, we don't need to be jerks about it. This is especially true in an age of instant communication, when it is so easy to fire off an angry email or text without taking the time to think it through, to re-read, to check our tone.

So, I vent to my journal ... all of the raw, unedited, *hurt-feelinged* venom. Once I'm more balanced, I can determine whether a situation actually needs to be addressed (which, if we're living whole-heartedly and with healthy boundaries, some *do* need to be addressed).

Pro-tip: don't type in the email address until you're content with the way you've communicated. Hitting "send" before intended is a nightmare. I know this from experience.

※

How about you, friend? What's weird and quirky about you?

Exhortative

(Life Hacks)

Chapter 32

Lighten the Load

"How can we drop negativity, as you suggest? By dropping it. How do you drop a piece of hot coal that you are holding in your hand? How do you drop some heavy and useless baggage that you are carrying? By recognizing that you don't want to suffer the pain or carry the burden anymore, and then letting go of it."

ECKHART TOLLE

A couple of mornings ago, I picked up my daughter's backpack to move it from one room to another. I was appalled at the weight of it. For interest's sake, I decided to see how much it actually weighed. First I weighed myself (and cringed, because quarantine baking and daily drinks are catching up with me). Then I put the backpack on, weighed myself again, and found the difference. As a storyteller, I am wont to exaggerate, but here, there is no need. The backpack weighed more than twenty pounds! That's almost a quarter of my daughter's total body weight!

The shocking thing is that my 14-year-old daughter hoists that school bag onto her back and walks around with it like it weighs nothing. She's used to it. She's grown accustomed to the weight. But that doesn't mean it isn't hurting her.

We all carry around heavy backpacks without even realizing the weight of them. When we add one sheet of paper at a time, we don't notice the incremental building. Until we do. Until it starts to be uncomfortable. Until it starts to cause us pain in other ways. Until we can't carry it anymore.

In our culture, we have rituals for decluttering, for sorting, for Marie-Kondo-ing. But these practices are typically for our physical spaces. Periodically, we sort through our kids' closets to remove items they've outgrown, or to eliminate socks with holes. About once a year, in a total rage, I throw away plastic containers without matching lids. In the springtime, we might corral items deemed 'no longer useful' for yard sales or donation pick-ups. We regularly purge our plastic, paper, and bottle recycling by placing it in defined bins, and then delivering it for roadside pick-up or to the nearest depot.

But we don't seem to have useful rituals for emotional or mental decluttering. In the same way we collect *stuff,* we also pick up feelings, absorb experiences, and store traumas. And without intention, there's nowhere for them to go. We just keep cramming them in. There's no yard sale for hurt feelings. There's no roadside pick-up for grief.

Back to the backpack. I have often used a backpack as a means of illustrating how easily we collect and carry heavy things. When I'm disappointed about something, it's as though a little stone goes into my backpack. Someone hurts my feelings, and another heavy rock is added. Constantly worried about money? Pebbles, pebbles, and more pebbles in my backpack. Individually, they may not weigh much, but collectively, they become heavy.

If we don't stop from time to time to purge or empty our packs, we'll carry around weight we were not meant to carry. We will grow accustomed to a heaviness that doesn't need to be there. We'll damage ourselves without even realizing.

One of my regular rituals is to pause and take stock. I empty my metaphorical backpack onto the ground and intentionally release each stone. This might mean letting someone off the hook for an insensitive comment, or forgiving myself for blundering with my words, or identifying and acknowledging a burr under my saddle. As I do this, I visualize placing the stones in a pile.

If one could see—if *I* could see—my life journey, one would observe a pathway or a trajectory marked with little stone alters all along the way. Altars are typically places of sacrifice where we lay hard things down. They can also be places of remembering, to mark a moment or an event. So, I take those heavy rocks—the hurts, the disappointments, the grief—and I intentionally remove them one by one from my soul. I name them, and I place them on the ground, one on top of the other, until a small altar is formed. And then I move forward with a considerably lightened load.

Earlier this week, I became conscious that I was feeling weighted again, that it was time to sift through my soul and build another altar. I sat with my eyes closed and asked what was happening inside of me. Because of the way life has been this last while, I have grown very adept at digging in when the weighted feelings come. Even when I don't feel like it (does anyone ever *feel* like it?). I was fully prepared for yet another funeral pyre. I was expecting to do the onerous work of grieving, of sacrificing, of letting go. But the scene in my mind unfolded differently.

I pictured myself hunched slightly, but grittily soldiering on along the path, like always. I was managing(-ish) all of my heavy things: large rocks in my hands, heavy items in my backpack, and crushing weights on my shoulders. In the scene in my mind, my companion—who, for me, is God or Spirit—urged me to slow and invited me to unload the burdens. I consented and my companion began easing the heavy things from my clenched fingers, my tired shoulders, my heavy heart ... and began building something.

Stone by stone, a familiar structure took shape beside me. I wasn't sure what would be sacrificed. Honestly, I don't know what I have left to sacrifice. But then my companion said, *No ... sit down, I'm making a meal. We're going to eat together and rest.* I recognized it was not a funeral pyre, but a cooking surface. Seated and relaxed by the small pile of hard things, we nourished ourselves. And then I laid down and slept.

The hard things became the means by which my strength was restored. I dreaded building another funeral pyre, but it wasn't about death. I steeled myself to allow forgiveness, but it wasn't about letting anything go. It was about eating, living, savoring, enjoying, resting. My companion repurposed my hard things as a vehicle for nourishment.

In this unusual and unprecedented phase of life, where only essential services are open, let's develop our own rituals for determining what is essential to our restoration, our wholeness, and our peace, joy, and love. We're in the process of stripping away so many things away right now because we have to. While we're at it, let's also Marie-Kondo the hell out of our inner lives. Let us intentionally purge the non-essentials and lighten our loads.

Unload the stones. Build an altar. Nourish yourself. Rest.

Chapter 33

Looming Shadows

"Sometimes you have to give yourself pep talks. Like "Hello. You're a badass...don't be sad, you got this, and I love you."

UNKNOWN

Ugh, I recognize this feeling. I know it well. It gives me flashbacks to university—that *something hanging over your head* feeling, that *dreading a due date* feeling. But not being able to get to it just yet, because there are sixty-five other things in the queue ahead of it.

I'm living in the shadow of a looming deadline.

The deadline was manageable from far off. I still had lots of time, so it was easy to *back-burner* it and address the other items first. But now, *this* is the next thing. *This* is the job that needs to be tackled. And I find myself somewhere between total paralysis and running and avoiding as though chased by some beast.

For the most part, I have learned to turn and face, head-on, jobs that need to be done. I used to avert my eyes and rush by the dishwasher full of clean dishes, begging to be unloaded. Though it was a five-minute job, I would spend sixty avoiding the task and praying someone else would do it before I finally got to it. Writing school report cards three times a year no longer ruins my life like it used to. With the implementation of good practices, like rewarding myself with candy, coffee, and Facebook breaks after each small goal is attained, the daunting task has been rendered palatable.

But *this* writing deadline I have approaching right now is kicking my butt! Sometimes writing ideas rush out of me like powerful rivers. The thoughts are born, formed, and ready. I love it when this happens, but it isn't always the case. More often, it's a gut wrenching, insecurity-inducing, dreadful act of will. Sheer perseverance akin to labor. It requires sitting your butt in the chair and refusing to move.

Though I've had thoughts and ideas floating around in my brain for the particular piece I need to produce, I've struggled to articulate it clearly. How am I going to say what needs to be said in 400 to 800 words? If you've read any of my essays, you will know this is near to impossible for me. My first pass was as exciting as a chapter from a psychology textbook. In the second attempt, I managed to completely undermine my own thesis statement. And so far, the third go is total crap. My confidence is shaken.

And so, I've been avoiding. Not entirely consciously, but yes, avoiding. Suddenly, I need to clean out my bathroom drawer because there are just way too many face mask samples filling up the space. And all of the baseboards in my house have a layer of dust that is, all at once, intolerable. And it is definitely time to purge my closet. And *"Hey kids, who wants banana-chocolate chip muffins?"*

And how about, instead of writing the *actual* essay that needs to be written, I write an essay about how I'm avoiding writing an essay?

How often do we do this in *all* parts of life? In avoiding a task—whether house maintenance, a difficult conversation, booking a doctor's appointment to address a medical concern—we allow the small thing to become a big thing. In avoiding what we're dreading, we end up enduring far more angst and stress than we would have done had we simply faced it in the first place.

Recently, while rehearsing for a difficult conversation that was on the near horizon, I experienced something like an expansive, dark shadow over and around me. Its borders were wide. I felt small in the middle of it. I felt fearful and tired as I huddled there in its darkness. And then I heard the words:

"The shadow looming is larger than the source. Turn and face it. See it for what it is."

When I turned around, I saw a surprisingly small tree. A small tree that was throwing a *very* large shadow. And here I'd wasted all this time cowering when the actual thing wasn't to be feared at all.

When we avoid something, we send ourselves the message that it is to be feared; we give it power over us. We unwittingly agree to become its victim. We give it permission to harass us and weigh heavily on us. But when we face it, we take back our control.

In the extreme, avoidance can present as numbing behavior, such as drinking too much, or eating too much, or sleeping too much, or watching too much television. When we notice that these parts of our life are out of balance, it's probably safe to assume there is something we are avoiding—a task, an event, or an issue that we don't want to face.

Maybe it's legitimately scary and overwhelming. Maybe you're avoiding medical tests because you would rather not know. Maybe you're avoiding having an honest conversation with your partner or spouse about an issue because you would rather sink than rock the boat. Maybe you're scrolling on Facebook instead of updating your resume because you're afraid to apply for that new job.

But it doesn't have to be something big—even small things can rub. Think of a pebble in your shoe! Maybe you're filling your time with trivial tasks that don't *really* need to be done right now because you're not sure how to begin the massive job. Maybe you're flipping through a trash magazine instead of opening the book you know will call you toward spiritual and emotional health.

Or maybe you're writing a different essay than the one that needs to be written. Touché.

I can't speak for you, but I know I've been giving the shadow power it doesn't deserve. Friends, let's turn around and look at the source; let's tame that thing looming over us. It's already wasted too much of our time and emotional energy. And it's probably not as big as we thought.

As for me, I'm going to pour another cup of coffee and lock myself away in my office. It's time to edit a 3000 word essay into an 800 word essay (barf).

We can do hard things. Say it with me: *We can do hard things!*

Chapter 34

Lean Hard

"Faith ... is the art of holding on to things your reason has once accepted, in spite of your changing moods."
C.S. LEWIS

There is a full spectrum between the benchmarks of extreme risk-taking (aka foolhardy) and extreme risk-avoidance (aka fearful). Wherever you identify on the foolhardy-fearful spectrum, we must all trust what is unseen. Whether it's that an elevator has been well-maintained by the people purporting to do so, or that our car brakes will slow us when we apply them, or that the pilot knows how to land this plane, or that a promise will be kept, or that God exists—it all requires faith.

I'm a risk-taker in the *small r, small t* sense of the word. I love adventure—trying new foods, exposure to diverse experiences and situations, exploring new cultures and languages, singing in front of crowds. Even when I'm uncomfortable and must control my shallow, nervous breathing, I actually like and seek change. But all of the risk-taking and adventure falls within some very defined boundaries. I enjoy risk on a firm foundation, preferring to control against any unpleasant consequences, like physical discomfort, or bankruptcy, or death.

Unlike people who embark on activities that could actually cause them harm, I'm the kind of person that likes a safety net. I want the thrill, but it needs to be a *safe* thrill.

Each time I get on a roller coaster, I have to remind myself that if people were *actually* dying on this ride, it wouldn't be allowed to remain open for the public. Whatever the activity, I like to know that I'm securely fastened, that the fear factor is *only for fun* and that I won't actually die.

I'm also a wee bit timid when it comes to entrepreneurial endeavours. Some people are motivated by risk; they have incredible business ideas, love being their own boss, putting it all on black, and knowing that it's up to them to make it work. I, on the other hand, do *not* want "the buck" (what even is a "buck"?) to stop with me. I like to know there's a paycheck coming on pay day. I don't actually want my great ideas to bankrupt me.

As for deck railings, I unconsciously give them a small push before placing my full weight against them, particularly if I'm higher than the first story. I, also, really appreciate the netting around our trampoline because when I, or one of the kids, get double-bounced, we throttle against the net and then fall back to the trampoline … instead of ending up in a nearby tree with a broken back. Call me wimpy, but I don't actually want to experience discomfort.

Living with faith is in direct opposition to my preference for safety and certainty. I have an innate inclination to control *all* of the circumstances; so, here's the annoying thing about faith. We don't get to set the guidelines. We don't get to see how it will all turn out and *then* decide whether or not to join or continue. We don't get to put parameters on risk, as in "I will do this *if* I am surrounded by protective netting." The minute we attempt to make faith certain, it's no longer faith.

Even if we *were* asked to run the show, we couldn't truly be trusted. My particular feelings on what is safe or not safe may alter day to day, depending on how much sleep I've had, the circumstances of my life, and how I read and filter situations through my mood. As much as I want to set the boundaries, I know I can't really be trusted to draw perfect lines. Instead, my faith (as relates to *everything*) is in a God who doesn't tire and doesn't experience mood swings, who is unchanging, always good and always wise. So I lean in this direction, despite my fickle emotions.

Faith in a God we don't see with our physical eyes sounds foolhardy. It sounds downright moronic. Stupid, even. Just as we wouldn't lean over the edge of a tall building to see how far we can go before forfeiting equilibrium, why would *anyone* lean into the invisible and intentionally put their faith in something or someone they cannot see?

And yet, for me, my richest life has always been when I lean hard into God. This girl who feels cynical about the reliability of your ropes and carabiners when rock climbing has somehow learned to throw her full weight on the unseen Divine. This girl who prefers a sure thing has learned to listen and act, even in unusual circumstances, to Love who can be trusted to give good counsel. This girl who would happily write her own story were she able, relinquishes full control to the author who has the best, most fulfilling life for her.

My safety in this life doesn't come by my own doing. With age and experience comes the startling realization that we actually have very little control of anything. Yes, we can obviously make wise choices for spiritual, physical, intellectual, and emotional health, yet ultimately, we are not in control. And so, we can live in fear or we can live in love.

Fearful living is small and inhibited. In *Life Lessons*, Elisabeth Kübler-Ross and David Kessler write that *"fear doesn't stop death, but stops life."*[1] Sadly, it *is* possible to be alive on this earth, doing all of the daily things that make us seem alive, but be dead. Conversely, living in love means we live with abandon; we peel our clenched fingers from the railing and trust that Love will do what Love does, proving it to us again and again.

Though I'm hesitant to lean hard against an unsecured railing, I somehow lean hard on Love. Love, who does not promise an absence of difficulty, but promises to be with us, and to be solid ground under our feet when the world feels shaky. Love who promises to be with us in decisions and guides us toward plans that are good. Love who offers comfort in pain and peace in anxiety.

I could go on ad nauseum, but instead, I'll bequeath the treasure hunt to you. Dig in and uncover the promises. Risk falling against these safety nets in this crazy world. Lean hard on these railings that keep us from tumbling over.

C.S. Lewis said, *"Relying on God has to begin all over again every day as if nothing had yet been done."*[2] So if you've never experienced Love's presence, or if it's been a while since you engaged your faith, begin all over again. Lean hard.

Love has held true for this risk-averse cynic, and I believe Love will hold true for you.

Chapter 35

On This Day

"Photography takes an instant out of time,
altering life by holding it still."

DOROTHEA LANGE

I love photographs. Before the age of the iPhone, I did not leave home without a real-life camera in my pocket or handbag. If you're as old as me, you'll remember the unbearable time lapse between sending off your "film" by mail (that's when you put something in an actual mailbox) and awaiting the return of your precious photos … unsure, even, if any of them will have turned out.

I am not a fabulous photographer, but I've always valued capturing moments. I adore fine photography, but for me, that isn't the point. I'm a *memory keeper*.

One of my favorite Facebook functions is "On This Day." I love reminiscing about what happened on this day three years ago, seven years ago, twelve years ago. With a visual aid, memories come rushing back in a detailed manner that my thoughts alone couldn't manage.

Recently, a video from more than a decade ago resurfaced, causing me to laugh explosively like I did when it happened. It was an early,

East Coast Canadian spring, and my then five-year-old son and three-year-old daughter had worked tirelessly to transfer freezing-cold, dirty water from the ditch, one plastic bucket-full at a time, into a small, plastic swimming pool—and then, they went "swimming." My voice can be heard in the background of the video, laughing and debating whether I'm a super-awesome mom or a negligent mom for allowing this to happen.

Images frozen in time are precious, but I've been thinking about how they can also be dangerous in terms of memory and perception. That *one* moment captured can determine how we remember events or reactions. Positively or negatively.

A facial expression can be captured that assigns a particular feeling to a memory that may only have been fleeting.

Maybe we remember someone as snarky or sullen because of the way they were frozen in that moment.

A brief moment is captured and remembered though it was truly inconsequential to the larger story.

Or maybe we fondly remember a person who wasn't *that awesome* most of the time.

We are more than our moments. Our moments make up our larger story, but they are not the *whole* story.

I am embarrassed to admit this out loud, but occasionally, I run into people that I knew in my younger years and immediately, a memory (a snapshot of who they were *then*) returns to me. With maturity, I know that they have likely grown to become whole, wonderful people. But what I remember is that one thing. That one misstep. That one rumor. That one snapshot.

We have to be careful not to *limit* people to snapshots. We must remember that we ourselves are not snapshots. We are all moving pictures. The moments that occur are not the end of the story, they are *part* of the story. If we freeze-frame, we'll capture perceptions that are not true of the whole.

We also need to be careful that we don't identify ourselves by small moments in our pasts.

Yes, I was a moody teenager at times, but I was also funny and delightful.

Harsh, thoughtless responses have certainly exited my mouth in difficult situations, but I am not harsh and thoughtless.

Maybe you have logged days, weeks and even years of recovery, only to relapse, but you are not forever lost.

We have walked through dark, painful seasons where hope has been little more than a flickering flame, but we are not hopeless.

We have tried and we have failed, but we are not failures.

The individual moments do not define us. They are parts of the larger story. A story where we are falling *forward*. Where, regardless of the steps backwards, we continue to gain ground.

As humans, we do not have the capacity to extract ourselves from time and space, to take a far enough step back from the timeline to see everything in the context of the larger story. But I believe God does.

God is outside of time, able to observe our individual moments. God sees our wins and our losses. God sees our brilliant moments and our screw-ups. But we are never held hostage in the moment. We are *growing toward* and God is a witness and a proponent for who and what we are becoming.

Oh, how I want to adopt a similar stance! I desire to be that witness and supporter in the lives of the people I love.

Of course we don't want to take every sad and destructive detour along the way to wholeness, but when we *do* deviate, we don't memorialize the failure. We *are* going to fall. But let's keep falling forward.

It's imperative that we remind ourselves that snapshots don't tell the whole story.

Chapter 36

Be Honest, For the Love O' God!

"I decided that the single most subversive, revolutionary thing I could do was to show up for my life and not be ashamed."

ANNE LAMOTT

S unday mornings were angst-filled for me for many years of my life. Music has always undone me, worship music even moreso. As I would stand there in church, allowing the songs to wash over me, I would be repulsed and ashamed of myself for the ways I'd screwed up once again. In my mind, I would picture myself grovelling and apologizing, face-down on the ground before God's throne, the tension between my two selves tearing me apart.

I grew up in a faith-rich environment. My parents modeled what it meant to love Jesus and others every single day. I was surrounded by stories of God's faithfulness, exposure to real-life miracles, daily worship, and prayer. *But* I'm the oldest kid in my family—which means that I was the guinea pig child and the ground breaker for the rest of my siblings. Oh, and I'm also a pastor's kid. This means I spent *a lot* of time in church. On display. Behaving. Playing the game. Or, at least, trying to.

The problem is, I've always been a little spicy. And I've always found humor in inappropriate things. True story: I missed watching Disney on Sunday nights more often than not as a consequence for my uncontrollable laughter during the very operatic "special music" in morning services. Or for snickering hysterically with my siblings because one of us had moved in such a way on the wooden pew as to create a 'fart' noise (though we certainly wouldn't have used *that* word). We wore 'church clothes' to church. We were quiet and patient. And we certainly didn't steal craft supplies from the Kids' Church room. *Oh, wait…*

Though unintentional, it was reinforced for me early on, as I'm sure it was for many of you (raised in church or not) that there were a different set of behaviors and expectations for church *(and therefore God)* than elsewhere. It seemed that God liked tidy. God liked compliance. God liked quiet. God liked blind obedience. God liked nice.

It was a total set up for leading a double life, because nothing heaps on more shame than trying to be something you are not. I was a nice kid, but I was not *those* things. I really, truly loved God, but I felt like a fraud. I didn't fit the mold … unless, of course, the mold was the preacher's daughter in the movie *Footloose*.

Even with a rich spiritual foundation, my teenage years were difficult. I knew I had faith, but as an obsessive thinker, I had a lot of questions about what I was experiencing in the world, as compared to what I'd learned. It was a time of trying to navigate what I believed versus what my parents believed. Trying to stand on my own two feet spiritually. I wrestled, and questioned, and sifted *everything*. I partied hard, *and* I continued to talk to God about all of it. (If I'm honest, not much has changed!)

When I was nineteen years old, I had a moment of epiphany that forever changed me. During one of my grovelling-at-God's-feet sessions, begging for forgiveness for each of my deadly sins (Dante would have been scandalized), I heard Love's voice. It said, *"Ellen, I'm up here!"* As I looked up, I saw hands reaching for me, like a parent picking up a small child. I was gathered up and held closely.

After years of living shame-ridden—of feeling like I was straddling two worlds and that my life was incongruent—I felt whole. I was finally able to hear the words of affirmation being spoken to me. I was finally able to see the look of total loving acceptance in God's eyes. And forever since, this is where I picture myself: wrapped up by Love. Completely wanted. Completely safe. Completely loved. God is *not* a harsh critic who rubs our noses in our accidents, but a loving parent who longs to hold us.

A double life—living in constant fear of being found out—is angst-filled and exhausting. And absolutely *not* what Love intended for us. So I quit living a double life. I wanted to be real ... to be fully who I was *no matter* where I was, or who I was with. Regardless of expectation or location, whether at church, school, work, with strangers, or with friends.

I felt whole and united and fully myself. The relief was palpable.

I won't lie. There were certainly ramifications. As it turns out, many people *prefer* tidy, compliant, quiet, obedient and nice. And the thing is, healthy doesn't always look "nice." I would often picture myself like an organic banana, free from chemicals and pesticides. I may not have looked as pristine and blemish-free as the pretty, yellow bananas—I was slightly banged up and covered with spots—but I was delicious and so much healthier!

Once unified, I stopped pandering to expected rules, which looked like talking openly with anyone and everyone, or offering to pray for friends regardless of where we were—the university cafeteria or the

Irish pub where I worked part-time. It also meant that I voiced opinions and ideas at church that I'd previously kept to myself (and that some likely wished I would have continued keeping to myself). There were no "place rules" for my sailor-esque vocabulary. Churchy people thought I'd gone "off the rails" and some of my friends thought I'd become "super churchy." But, I didn't care. I'd never felt more loved.

And when we live *loved*, viscerally loved, we can love ourselves and love others. As human beings, we long to be known for who we are, and yet, we are so easily repulsed and offended by *messy*. But true intimacy hinges on being completely real—we can't have healthy relationship without it ... with one another or with the Divine.

The result is that I am crazy honest with God. Like putting-it-*all*-out-there, no-holding-back, totally ugly, vulnerable honesty. I'm not super-spiritual or gifted or more *tight* with the Divine than anyone else. As is often my path, I've learned to be honest the hard way.

Raw honesty with God allows us to know immense security, deep down in our foundations. When we understand that Love wants us to be who we were created to be, with all of our emotions, eccentricities, quirks and yeah, even the occasional screw up that comes with having free will, we can begin to live fully.

We spend so much time and energy endeavouring to seem *put together* and *presentable* when *God's the one who knows us the best*. Love created us, knows us, loves us—every single part. No need for feigning. No need for hiding.

So, go ahead. Get honest. Ask your questions. Pour out your feelings. Say what you really think. You are loved more than you can ever know.

Chapter 37

Does Everyone Have Friends But Me?

"The most important things in life are the connections you make with others."

TOM FORD

Here's a vulnerable admission for you:

When I am overly-tired, overly-extended, and (god-forbid) overly-hormonal, my go-to insecurity and pet-sadness tends toward feeling like I don't have friends. While I know this is *entirely ridiculous*, it can *feel* really real.

How, with *so many* people in my everyday life, can I sometimes feel alone? How can I count so many people "friends" while still wondering occasionally if I have any friends?

As is usually the case, nature and nurture have contributed in equal parts. Some of my *friend angst* is by virtue of personality. I was born with the delightful propensity to overthink *everything*. Sometimes it serves me well, and often, not so much. As for nurture, I've pondered whether my early years may have contributed to feelings of disconnection more than I realized.

We moved around *a lot* my whole entire life. By the time I was twenty-five years old, I'd called approximately sixteen addresses *home*. That's three countries, three provinces, three elementary schools, one junior high, two high schools. I can't draw a consistent line of people who have been in my life from early on. It's more of a dotted line, made from multiple line segments. I have a wide swath of friends in individual servings and small pockets that span decades of my life and geographical locations.

I learned to be friendly and resilient, but I also question whether these gypsy beginnings may have adversely affected my sense of rootedness and connection. Or, maybe moving has nothing to do with it; it's simply a human feeling.

I've more accurately renamed this feeling in recent years; that it's not so much a case of *friendless*, but of feeling *disconnected*. And though it doesn't change the fact that I go ages without seeing friends, the semantic shift helps my heart.

There have been phases of life when I felt connected—like living in community in Europe while working with a missions organization. Like university, when I spent long hours with other students in my cohort. But this is *not* one of those naturally connected phases. It takes much more intentionality.

In this age of easy access to real-time posts and images, it can seem like everyone else is getting together all the time, going on trips together, meeting for coffee. Maybe we feel left out of events or friendships that we perceive to be thriving. But maybe the disconnection is *not* as a result of feeling left out because we weren't invited—it's a case of not being able to get there! Because we're home with sick babies. Because of work. Because of anxiety. Because we can't find a sitter.

Because of illness. Because of crappy weather. Because of the excessive driving that accompanies having tweens and teens.

When you throw in a little parenting, a full-time job, responsibilities and obligations, house work, that annoying human need to sleep and eat ... *voila*! Zero time remaining.

If I don't tend to my thoughts, this current phase of life can leave me feeling very disconnected. I'm around people all the time, but the quick, superficial conversations don't fill the need for deep friendship...the desire to know and be known.

One of my goals this year was to work through an older book called *The Artist's Way* by Julia Cameron about unblocking creativity and becoming the creatives we were meant to be. A particular quote about creativity actually convicted me on the level of friendship, specifically on the "I have no friends" lie.

I hope Ms. Cameron won't mind, but I've swapped out the 'creative' bits with friendship words.

> *"Indulging ourselves in a frantic fantasy of what our life would look like if we [had friends], we fail to see the many changes that we could make at this very moment. This kind of look-at-the-big-picture thinking ignores the fact that a [friend-rich life] is grounded on many, many small steps and very, very few large leaps...[friendship] requires activity and this is not good news to most of us. It makes us responsible, and we tend to hate that. You mean I have to DO something in order to [have friends]?"[1]*

And there it is. A plan of action. I can either sit in my house (or van) feeling alone and left out, *or* I can be intentional and take small steps to make new friends and to foster existing friendships.

Rather than large leaps, here are a few small ideas that have helped me arrest that friendless, isolated feeling.

I decided to break the insular, alone cycle by inviting people into our home for a meal once a month. It doesn't sound like much, but it's so much better than *never* (which can easily happen when you're not scheduling it on purpose). The result is that we've met many great people and have actually become closer friends with some of them. It doesn't have to be fancy! If you don't enjoy cooking, buy a roast chicken and a salad from the grocery store. Get a bottle of wine. While delicious food is certainly among my favorites, it's not about the food. It's about sitting at a table together and creating space for connection.

Another step that was built into my schedule for years was an accountability group. It was not an open group, which sounds terribly exclusive, but the intention was not to exclude. The reality is, in order to create safety, sometimes we have to walk closely with just a couple of people. These women and I committed to walking together in honesty so that we could grow spiritually and emotionally.

Because of the busyness of life, we met bi-weekly, come rain or shine, hell or high water (or husbands who forgot that it was *our* night). Sometimes it was fairly superficial and fun with snacks and story-telling (which *is* super important for connection). Sometimes we shared things we'd not shared with other humans and cried our eyes out. Sometimes we prayed for one another, sometimes we didn't. Sometimes we left feeling uplifted and gloriously supported, and sometimes we left feeling agitated and riled up because a nerve had been touched and we knew it was something we'd have to look at. This accountability group filled a need for deep connection.

Texting and social media save my life! It's no replacement for shared space and face-to-face conversation, but when that isn't an option, texting with friends helps me to remember I have friends. My baby group is a key example. We used to meet at least once a week, but now, thanks to those very babies that brought us together, it's more like every 6-8 weeks. So, in the interim, we have an almost daily group chat that ranges in topics from what to do with spiralized veggies, to whether bologna is a valid meal option, to parenting issues, to hilarious memes. It's not a substitute for real-time, but it helps.

I've also determined to get back on track with hosting simple soirées and brunches. It's something I've always enjoyed, but once again, when we're not doing it on purpose, suddenly two years go by ... and those friendless feelings come knocking. Brunch is not about the crepes with whipped cream and strawberry compote. It's not about the hot coffee. It's not about the cinnamon bread or the fresh berries. (*Gawd, I love food*). These things are exquisite and take the brunch experience right over the top, but the real reason brunch matters is *people*. People matter and brunch carves out space for people. Brunch creates space for connection.

Create a Facebook event. Make it a potluck so it's not all on your shoulders. Simply open your very normal home (that probably has dog-hair tumbleweeds blowing around and several loads of laundry on some surface waiting to be folded ... just like mine does) and create a space for people to connect.

Join a small group at your church. Show up at a Mother-Baby event. Call someone to meet you for coffee while you're waiting out your kid's hockey practice.

Instead of waiting to be invited, *invite!* Make the first move.

My hunch is that many of us experience the disconnected feeling, at least occasionally. To counter the friendless lie, we need to stop running from it. Turn around and face it. Because if we wait until we have time to pursue friendship, or until our house is perfect, or until someone extends an invitation to us ... we may very well find ourselves disconnected and lonely.

To foster a friend-rich life, decide on one small step and do it. And then, do it again. And again.

Chapter 38

Telephone-Pole-to-Telephone-Pole

—

"There's no there there."

GERTRUDE STEIN

—

Recently, there was a meme floating around on social media that I found to be hilarious. Probably because it's something I've actually said: "If you see me running, you'd better run, too, because there's probably something chasing me."

I *used* to be a runner. You're probably picturing someone wearing a merino wool base-layer with compression running tights. Maybe a light-weight shell and the latest running shoes with energy-return technology? Perhaps a look of sheer joy and freedom on my face? No. Wrong. Not me.

Though I ran for many years, I never experienced that *unicorn* people refer to as "runner's high." Instead of euphoria, I experienced nausea—feeling like I was going to die the entire time, every time. I was committed to it, but I hated it.

It was only ever light-weight apparel for me because a slight cool mist or a single flake of snow were enough reason to cancel. No need to buy winter running gear because where I live, slipping on ice or getting hit by a snowplow are very real possibilities—and not that appealing to me. Besides, running in the cold makes me cough. So I didn't run in the cold. Yes, I always had great sneakers, but that was about it. I was only running to stay fit. I was only running to get it over with. I was absolutely a telephone-pole-to-telephone-pole kind of girl.

About seven years ago, post-MRI, I was told "no more running." My knees were done. They had used up all of their cushion and could no longer handle any impact. While I grieved the loss of my cartilage and the diagnosis of severe osteoarthritis, I was secretly relieved that I *wasn't allowed* to run anymore. No more hustling. No turning up the music to drown out my own gasping. No more dragging my butt to the next telephone pole. I needed to find a new way to exercise.

As it turns out, the telephone-pole-to-telephone-pole technique wasn't unique to my running. For years, it was how I did life. I was convinced that if I could just make it to the next driveway, to the end of the street, to the stop sign, I'd be okay. In real terms, if I could just make it through this busy weekend, if I could get my report cards finished, if I could punch my list of things to do in the face, then I'd be able to rest. I would be happy once I met the right person, once I paid off this debt, once this dispute was settled. I'd have peace when promises were fulfilled, once I'd made it through another bedtime routine. I'd be less tired once my kids would sleep through the night, once hockey season was over, once the summer came. I'd be happy once I owned my own house, once I got a new car, once I had more time.

But as I heard someone quote recently, "there's no there *there*."[1] It's a moving target. A dangling carrot. A hazy oasis on the horizon.

Just as the knee issue necessitated a change that forced me to slow down, so the terrifying nightmare of a potentially missed life scared me awake. Changes needed to be made. My soul had used up all of its cushion and could no longer handle any impact. I was sick to death of bracing myself, of limping along, of just trying to make it through alive. In my journal, I wrote:

> "*I feel like I'm perpetually waiting for something. Waiting to get through this part, so that I can get on to the next thing. Waiting to finish school. Waiting for job security. Waiting for our house renovations to be completed. Waiting for the kids to stop fighting. Waiting until we pay off our debt. Waiting to get on with my life. Waiting to be meaningful. Waiting for things to be less stressful. Waiting until there is resolution. Waiting for the other shoe to drop. Waiting to get it all done. Waiting to live. Waiting to be myself. Waiting to have joy. Waiting to fully engage. Waiting to lock in with my life. Waiting for the hard part to be over. Waiting. Waiting. Waiting. And in the process of just trying to get through; just trying to make it—I'm missing it! I'm missing the life that I have!*"

The fear gave way to intentionality. I chose to accept that this is what life looks like; because if I didn't embrace it and enjoy it for what it was, I was going to miss it. What if I suddenly woke up at 100 years old? I would be filled with the worst kind of regret! A life unnoticed and under-appreciated. A life endured rather than a life lived.

And so, I learned to be glad in the midst of my busy, chaotic, sometimes heart-wrenching life. No more wasting it on waiting. No more plugging my ears and singing "la, la, la" to drown out the noise.

The shocking revelation that I was missing my life coincided with my discovery of Ann Voskamp's book *One Thousand Gifts*.[2] In it, she tells the story of how, after years of struggling with depression and grief, a friend dares her to write down one thousand reasons for which to be thankful. It changed her life. And it changed my life. I began practicing gratitude right there in the middle of the imperfect mess. I chose (yes, *chose*) to appreciate what life looked like, even when it was sometimes (often) hard.

Gratitude continues to be interspersed throughout my journals—I'm somewhere in the seven thousands now—and the entries range from single words to short paragraphs, and from the mundane (1335. I smell coffee!) to the powerful (3208. This battle is not mine to fight. Laying down my weapons and waiting for deliverance). Sometimes the gratitude flows easily and other times, I feel like I'm scraping the bottom of the outhouse to find one good thing.

I wish I could say that I've applied the lesson learned continuously since that time. As humans we're easily lulled into a numb state. We forget to stay awake, even though we may have already learned a particular lesson. That revelation that *so* impacted and changed us grows dim and we need a kick in the pants. I recently received such a kick.

One day, while singing at the top of my lungs—on stage in front of hundreds of people—I felt a divine boot connect with my rump. Instantly, I knew I'd slipped into old patterns of behavior. I was back to waiting again. I'd returned to putting my head down and running the gauntlet. Without even realizing it, I'd put my fingers back in my ears and was singing "la, la, la," waiting for it to be over. I'd hunched my body into a protective crash position that could handle impact and I was running like a maniac rugby player to get to the other side.

While externally, I continued to sing, internally, I stopped. And kneeled. I peeled my eyes from the horizon in order to be present right where I was. I used all of the heavy rocks I was carrying to build an altar. Right there in the middle.

Sometimes we think of an altar as a fancy table at the front of a church, or as a place of sacrifice, or maybe like the stone table in Narnia. The word origin indicates a place to worship, to sacrifice, and to commemorate what God has done. I'm not really *into* sacrificing live animals, but the heart behind it *is* something I'm into. The practice of placing something of value on the altar—a relinquishing that actually costs us. For me, it's my self-sufficiency, my effort, my control, my efficiency, my single-handed capacity to make it all work. An altar can be a place where we stop in the middle of whatever is happening and say, *Love, you are faithful. I trust you. Right here in the middle.*

And this is how we get *there*—to that elusive place we're straining toward. That finish line that doesn't actually exist. *This* is where true peace comes. By being thankful in the middle. Not by reaching the next telephone pole. And certainly not by making it across the finish line.

So, instead of gasping and enduring and hanging on until it's over, I'm responding, once again, to the invitation to stop. I'm exchanging labored running for intentional walking and frenzied hustling for thankful dependence. One by one, I'm laying down all of the heavy stones I'm carrying—my worries, my pain, my mis-guided attempts at controlling my life—but not haphazardly. I'm thoughtfully placing each one. As I lay each stone, I'm surrendering and remembering goodness. It's not once we get there...not only there on the other side. It's right here, right now.

Chapter 39

Keeping It Real IV

I've always wanted to be a laid-back, easy-going person, to have the kind of presence that would cause others to remark: "She is SO innately peaceful and lovely to be around." But, have you met me? I am SO the very opposite of that! I'm as intense, and *too much*, and type-A as they come. And though maturity and grace do tame my many opinions and passionate responses to situations, this IS who I am.

❋

Jokes stress me right out. When somebody begins to tell a joke, I am immediately angst-ridden, waiting for the punchline, knowing I'm not going to think it's funny, but that I'm going to be expected to respond in an appropriate manner, like laughing or snorting. I do not mean that I don't like humor… I *love* humor, but the things that make me laugh tend to be a little darker in nature. Shocking, I know. Some of my all-time favorites are "Deep Thoughts"[1] by Jack Handy, and also, memes. Seriously, why are memes so funny?

❋

I am perplexed by people who seem able to float along life's surface, perpetually buoyant. Conceivably, it's by nature of their personality type, or equally likely, I've fallen prey once again to the myth of shiny paint. As one who is highly sensitive and who feels everything deeply, I'm sometimes envious of those whom I perceive to be unaffected (though I know, in reality, there are actually about zero people in this category). Surely *they* just hide the hard stuff or manage it better than I do. In any case, I am not one of these people.

I am in the thick of it. I feel every single jarring step, every blow, every unintentional slight. I sometimes feel like I'm slogging, waist-deep, through swampy terrain, or like I'm in a video game where the goal is to dodge flying debris—duck and weave or endure constant collisions.

Being sensitive and feeling deeply makes life harder, for certain, but it also forces me to go deep. Though I occasionally complain and rail against hardship, I would not change my journey. I have learned to war. I have learned to know peace. I have learned to live with deep joy in the middle of the mess.

※

Hey, friend? One more thing. You are so loved. Exactly as you are.

Cyclical

(Learning and Relearning)

Chapter 40

New Year's Resolution

"May you be happy. May you be well. May you be peaceful and at ease. May you be filled with loving kindness and compassion for all beings."

MORIHEI UESHIBA

January 1st has got *nothin'* on September. January gets all the glory, with its fancy hats and blowers and prosecco toasts, but September is the *legitimate* new year; it's the actual starting line.

September fills me with anticipation. It's GO time! It's launch season! It's the stage for resetting goals, reframing what the year will look like and putting new systems in place (however short-lived; I guess we'd best keep January as a back-up plan). I feel invigorated and expectant, ready to return to routine—all the while aware of what lies ahead. My excitement is tempered with reality, for although I adore this time of year, I also have to steel myself. I must call on my grit, take deep breaths, possibly carb-load … and face the gauntlet.

Life is busy. Very busy. For all of us. Whether we're surrounded by kids or we're living solo, our schedules are at capacity. My personal phase of life happens to include full-time work as a school teacher, an unbelievable amount of time in hockey rinks, a substantial relationship with my school community, a passionate commitment to writing, and several hours each week at a horseback riding arena (I am camped out in the back seat of my vehicle right now, squeezing in writing time, while my daughter tacks up a horse inside the barn. For real). I really love *all* of the things, and it vexes me that time is finite, that there is only so much. We simply cannot manipulate or elongate the hours in a day, and so, it often feels like there isn't enough time.

Except that there is.

Good Earth's Sweet and Spicy tea is one of my absolute favorites. I can't buy it where we live, so whenever I'm away, I pick up a few boxes. Beyond the inexplicable deliciousness of the tea, there are these lovely, little quotes on the tea bag tags. The last tag I read offered a timely message to arrest my September gauntlet preparations:

"When God made time, he made enough of it." (Celtic saying)

I walked around for days afterwards, pondering these words and speaking them out loud to myself. Time was organized into days and nights and called good. They say that God does all things well, so if there's no scrimping or miscalculating to blame, clearly, *I* have been doing something wrong. I have been letting the tail wag the dog, as *they* say. I have been going too easily with the flow and have been carried along with the current. Not this year, baby!

Some years ago, I underwent a rigorous, informal education in setting priorities and in learning to say *no*. It was really hard for me. My personality is such that I can muster passion for just about anything, and everything seems like a brilliant opportunity in the moment. For years, I had myself spread paper thin, and those who should have been getting the best of me, including myself, were getting leftovers. In response to Love's invitation to do what was *only mine to do*, I became adept at setting boundaries and declining offers that didn't adhere to said priorities. The parts that remain in my life now are there *on purpose* or cannot be cut out (because, as it turns out, my family still wants to be fed. Sheesh). The pace can be staggering, but for the most part, even in exhaustion, I embrace it. But I want more than to survive these busy years. I want to thrive.

My word for this season is *ease*. Identifying a theme word is not something I've done before; the choosing was not intentional. I simply noticed one day, while scanning through journal entries, that "ease" was written countless times. There were gratitude entries, thankful for the *ease* with which an event had occurred or the *ease* with which words had flowed during a potentially difficult conversation. The word was also present in many written prayers, desiring that solace that ease embodies. On recognizing the pattern in my writing over the course of a few weeks, I felt compelled to pay attention, to give *ease* some deeper thought.

My first thought was that ease doesn't necessitate a change of external circumstances, but that the way we move through the event changes. Metaphorically, I see it like this. It's the difference between struggling against the water—chest-deep in a raging river, half-drowned, gasping for breath and exhausted by the current ripping my feet from beneath me—and diving under. Though the rapid-riddled surface keeps raging and the current keeps pulling, I slide smoothly under the water into the quiet. Instead of soldiering on, forcing my way upstream against a current that wants to wash me away, I dive under and slide more easily through the water—less resistance, less friction.

For me, this looks like partnering with Love and walking through every single moment of my day in the knowledge that I am not alone. I am covered. I am loved. I dive under and engage all things with joy, even the menial stuff. On the surface, it may appear that nothing has changed. But my experience of situations changes remarkably.

Another thought was that ease *does not* mean easy. Easy evokes escapism, pretending everything is A-okay and bobbing superficially along the surface. Easy wants mountain tops and no valleys, refusing to acknowledge that life can actually be simultaneously difficult *and* beautiful. When we believe things should be easy, we end up frustrated, disappointed and cynical, because they rarely are. Easy lacks depth and nuance, whereas ease feels like grace.

Ease offers sanctuary in the eye of the storm. Ease indicates a lightening or lessening of concern, struggle and discomfort. Ease feels like sliding through life's circumstances un-rocked, unafraid, unaffected by the waves. Let the storms swirl and rage, you'll find me sipping my coffee or napping. Ease doesn't mean things are easy, it means we are at peace, even when circumstances are not because we know Love calms the storms.

So, my September New Year's resolution is this: *I will navigate this year with ease.* Instead of hanging on for dear life, enduring all that the schedule demands, I'm going to dive under every day. I'm going to embrace work and meetings and hockey games and practices and rehearsals and meals and driving and driving and driving from a place of peace.

Even when life isn't easy, I'm choosing to live with ease.

Chapter 41

A Nasty Case of the Februarys

---

*"In times like these, it is good to remember that
there have always been times like these."*

PAUL HARVEY

Early one morning, I sat quietly with my coffee, preparing my
heart for the day with prayer and journaling. I opened my beautiful, turquoise journal and wrote:

"God, I. Am. Effing. Ornery. I've had enough sleep. There are no
sinister hormones at large. There is nothing awry on which to hang
these feelings. I don't know what's wrong with me! I'm irritable, edgy,
and I feel like I have no skin on. The facade remains falsely intact—
smile plastered on and voice controlled—but I feel short-fused and
scary on the inside, biting my tongue to near metaphorical severing.
I hate all of our animals with their furniture-scratching claws and
floor-muddying paws. I hate dishes in the sink. I hate melting, dirty
snow with dead grass peeking through. I hate germ-ridden, coughing
humans. I hate fifty thousand events on the calendar. I hate random,

dirty socks tucked behind couch cushions. I hate appointments running late. I hate *all of the things*."

Sorry, is that not what you were expecting? Ha!

I believe that God knows my every thought and feeling before I've even thought it or felt it, so I'm safe and can be 100% honest about *everything*. Which means that, sometimes, I'm filled with soft words and flowers and butterflies, and sometimes, venom. God accepts all of it, loves the gentle, thankful me *and* the complaining, messy me.

A few lines later, I had a moment of awareness. *"Wait a minute. This sounds familiar … didn't I write this exact same thing last year? And maybe the year before that? Oh geez! I've got a case of "the Februarys!"*

No offense to February. Maybe February is lovely where you live (if so, insert your own dreary season here). On the North-Eastern coast of North America, February is gross. It's a trickster, acting like the shortest month of the year, when really, it *feels* like the longest. While some of you may have birdsong and daffodils, we have slush, dirty snow and freezing cold temperatures. We are still approximately one hundred years away from springtime.

"The Februarys" leave me feeling foggy and burdened. Even if I've miraculously had enough sleep, I wake up exhausted and counting how many hours remain until I can crawl back into bed. I long for sunshine and warmth and suffer my jealousy quietly as others discuss vacation plans South for spring break.

I can often recognize a case of "the Februarys" in that vague sense that something isn't right. While I usually agree with Julian of Norwich that *"All shall be well, and all shall be well, and all manner of thing shall be well,"*[1] February finds me embodying the antithesis: All is *not* well, and all *will not* be well, and all manner of things will *never* be well. Delightful, right?

The melancholy onslaught actually took me by surprise this year. Normally, I'm prepared for it. I hunker down, hibernation-ready, determined to power through this dark, cold season of ours. But we've had such a wimpy, haphazard winter by our regular standards, with temperatures vacillating drastically, that I'm convinced I was thrown off my game.

Extremes make me ready and alert—but the middle *'non'* place puts me to sleep. With less snow and warmer temperatures, I became apathetic and didn't notice "the Februarys" drawing near.

But now I see you, blah-February feelings, and I'm recalibrating. I'm waking up and I'm back on course. I may have lagged in the middle, but I'll be finishing strong!

How do we finish strong when we're winter-weary, dulled and overwrought? When the usual things of life feel exhausting? When the fog is so pea-soup thick that the path disappears? What then?

First of all, we simply recognize "the Februarys" for what they are: feelings. Dreary, tired, slogging feelings. And feelings are *not* the boss of us. We can feel all of these things and still get out of bed. Still go to work. Still love our people. Still love ourselves. Acting kinder than we feel does not make us inauthentic—it's *not* faking, it's choosing. (Seasonal depression would fall under a different category of treatment than what is being suggested here).

Next, we keep going. We stick to the plan. We don't deviate off course, adjust the coordinates, or apply major changes. While minor course corrections are inevitable as we move toward a set goal, it's dangerous to completely alter our plans based on a case of "the Februarys." If your plan was to sail from point A to point B, keep working that plan. Clear weather is a better time for "re-calculating."

And finally, we do the next right thing. This precept of Alcoholics Anonymous and myriad other counseling and self-help programs invites us to adopt a manageable, step-by-step approach to overwhelm. Instead of seeing the whole, massive list of things to do, complete the next right thing. Instead of fearing the mountain to be scaled, look for the next safe foothold.

Sometimes the next right thing looks like turning off Netflix and going to bed a half hour earlier. Sometimes it means pouring another cup of coffee and lounging reflectively for ten more minutes before the rush. Sometimes it means sitting your butt down and writing that hard email you've been avoiding. None of this is earth-shattering revelation, but with "the Februarys" in play, we sometimes forget. We risk choking if we attempt to swallow the proverbial elephant whole.

My journal entry ended that day with a prayer of gratitude:

> *"God, thank you for helping me to name this; for helping me to recognize it for what it is, so that I don't give it more power than it deserves. Help me now to do the next right thing; to keep putting one foot in front of the other until, suddenly, instead of dirty snow and a half-hibernated brain, I feel warm sunshine and clarity."*

No offense, February—you're beautiful in your own way—but I'm happy your turn is almost over for another year. Soon, the darkness will lift and we'll enter a new season, literally and metaphorically ... and I cannot wait.

Chapter 42

Autumnal Reflections: What Needs to Go?

"If it's not a HELL YES, it's a no."

JEN HATMAKER

Imagine, if you will, me standing in my kitchen late at night, surrounded by mountains of cucumbers and tomatoes that I grew in my own garden, making pickles and salsa for my family, crying my eyes out with exhaustion because I have to wake up again in a few hours for my real, full-time job. And feeling SO mad that I can't do it all.

Hi, my name is Ellen, and I am compulsively responsible.

I have an overdeveloped sense of responsibility and commitment—a tendency to try to do it all. I could blame it on various factors: my intense, achiever personality or birth-order (*yes, I'm a firstborn. Shocking.*) or life experience (*the need to step up at an early age*). However, nature and nurture aside, this seemingly positive trait is one I've had to wrestle with and grow through.

When I give my word, I follow through. When I say I'll be there, I'll be there. When I agree to something, barring natural disaster or illness, you can count on me! I typically don't promise anything unless I'm certain I can make it happen because I feel the weight and responsibility of my *yeses*.

While commitment and responsibility *are* admirable qualities in many respects, and certainly, markers of good character, it *can* go too far. As is often the case, our best qualities and our worst qualities are one and the same, two sides of the same coin. Some people need to learn to show up and keep their word, and others, like me, may need to learn to relax a little.

Over the last few years, I've understood that the best version of me isn't the one who says yes to every invitation ... even if I *can* do it ... even if it's an honorable and meaningful opportunity ... even if I sometimes *want* to do it. What's scary is that I can muster passion for just about anything, so I can't always count on my feelings to guide me in whether or not something is mine to do.

My desire to help others, to step up, to show up, and to be counted trustworthy can easily cause me to overextend myself. I can collect and collect and collect and carry and carry and carry to the point that my arms are overfull and I'm exhausted.

It's not meant to be that way.

The truth is, we *cannot* keep picking up new things without putting others down. And if we don't *put things down* purposefully and intentionally, we'll *put them down* by accidentally "dropping the ball," as they say; unintentionally sacrificing something or someone that wasn't meant to be dropped.

As much as I'd like to believe I have an immeasurable capacity for work and people and life, annoyingly, I do have limits. I hate to admit it, even to myself, but I *cannot*, in fact, do all of the things. At least not simultaneously. At least not with any degree of quality. At least not without causing suffering to myself and others.

Some years ago, I experienced a necessary re-ordering of priorities. It was a time when everything in my life seemed to be vying for attention. It was the *tyranny of the urgent*, where the most persistent and most needy tended to get my best. Often at a cost to me and a detriment to my people. Everything I was doing was important and worthwhile, but instead of getting my best, *my people* were getting the leftovers. I was giving it all away to the loudest voices and bringing home scraps.

And so, I made a list of the important things in my journal and then drew a diagram (remember, friends, *I am a nerd*).

My commitment to Love comes first. Before you gasp with disbelief that I would choose faith over my family, *it's not like that.* We're not talking 'pieces of the pie' here where unequal slices are being served. With the divine as the inner circle, it doesn't mean that other parts get ignored, but that Love is at the center of everything. Everything I do after that … loving myself, loving my family, loving the world … comes from this centered place.

Next circle, partner. Again, this is not saying that my person gets a bigger slice of the pie than the babies who grew in my body. It's saying that loving him well and making our relationship a priority contributes to everything else. If my person and I are not okay, this typically affects all the other things. There is a trickle-down effect, and I want it to be a good one. You've likely heard the saying "Dads, the best thing you can do for your kids is to love their mom. Moms, the best thing you can do for your kids is to love their dad." I believe this to be true. Prioritizing your relationship with your partner creates security and peace for your children. And you.

The next circle is my kids. After that, family and close friends. And after that, my acts of service. This would include service to others, special projects I take on when called to do so, my giving and service "jobs" and so forth. (A side note: Friends, do not confuse what you *DO* for your faith with your relationship with the divine. Service comes out of your love for God; it is not one and the same). And after that, everything else.

This diagram of concentric circles became my measuring stick for everything. If an activity from an outer circle was usurping the place of my family, I would have to stop and re-order. And sometimes eliminate.

So, how does this happen? How do we re-order and/or eliminate items from our lists?

I've become aware that I've unconsciously assigned beginnings to the bright and beautiful category and dismissed endings to a list that also contains words like sadness, fading, dissolution, and failure to thrive. As though an ending means loss. As though an ending means something has gone wrong. As though an ending is to be avoided.

But we know this is impossible. One cannot possibly have *all* beginnings and *no* endings. What would that look like? How could that even work? The simple answer is *it doesn't*. We end up with **too many things**.

There are cycles and seasons in every part of the natural world. Plants cycle through seed, germination, growth, pollination, and seed spreading stages. Trees experience spring growth where they wake up and burgeon with new bud, then full leaf and summer slow-down, before fading to falling leaf and winter dormancy. The moon waxes and wanes through eight phases almost monthly. Tides rise and fall daily. Animal migration, tied to seasons, weather and feeding patterns, or mating and breeding, happens at regular intervals. Other animals hibernate each year. The gestation period from conception through birth has a beginning and an ending. Seasons begin and end, fading from one into the next.

As humans who are a part of the natural world, it follows that these same cycles, patterns, and seasons would exist in our own experience. So why are we often so surprised by endings? Why do we avoid them?

The song "Turn! Turn! Turn!" made famous by The Byrds is actually a scripture from Ecclesiastes[1]:

> *"There is a time for everything,*
> *and a season for every activity under the heavens:*
> *a time to be born and a time to die,*
> *a time to plant and a time to uproot,*
> *a time to kill and a time to heal,*
> *a time to tear down and a time to build,*
> *a time to weep and a time to laugh,*
> *a time to mourn and a time to dance,*
> *a time to scatter stones and a time to gather them,*
> *a time to embrace and a time to refrain from embracing,*
> *a time to search and a time to give up,*
> *a time to keep and a time to throw away,*
> *a time to tear and a time to mend,*
> *a time to be silent and a time to speak,*
> *a time to love and a time to hate,*
> *a time for war and a time for peace."*

While we would like to assign many of these items to categories of positive and negative, desirable or to be avoided, they are all valid and necessary parts of the human experience. Things must begin and things must end.

A long-term, enduring "yes" is important to certain aspects of life, like covenants of marriage and vows to love and protect our children. But perhaps not all parts of life require that level of commitment? Maybe some parts follow the natural patterns and are more cyclical than we'd like to believe?

Let's think on our priorities and ask what needs to be re-ordered or removed:

1) What things in your life need to lie dormant or hibernate for a season? Trees don't die when they lose their leaves, just as animals don't die when they hibernate. Both are very much alive, but not awake. It's how they pass through certain seasons. Putting something on the shelf, like allowing soil to rest fallow, can restore fertility and life.

2) What things in your life have died or need to die? This is a more difficult question, but, truly, there are parts of life that are only meant for a time. It seems tragic, but not all jobs, passions, relationships, or commitments are meant to endure. Longevity doesn't always equate to winning and shorter seasons don't always equate to losing. We need to recognize when something is over. Stop propping it up and let it go.

Autumn is a natural waning time, both in nature and metaphorically. If you're in a season of ending, it's not that the thing wasn't meant to be, or that it will never know life again. It just means that this part is over. At least for now. Circle of life, baby. Let it go.

Chapter 43

Sabbatical

"*Almost everything will work again if you unplug it for a few minutes...including you.*"

ANNE LAMOTT

Weird metaphors started repeating in my mind, like "I am biscuit dough rolled too thin" or "I am too much bread with too little butter," and I knew I had better pay attention. Activities I usually loved to do held little appeal, indicating it was time to pull back. My soul was demanding silence, solitude, and release from the many responsibilities (both chosen by me and assigned to me). It was time to unclench my fingers from the steering wheel of my own life.

Though, typically, I maintain a high level of self-care, the busyness of my work, a hectic family schedule, finishing a longer-than-planned house flip, sustained relational strain, and life generally, all left me depleted. Physically & emotionally.

There is actually a finite amount of time and energy allotted to us. We cannot keep adding new activities and responsibilities—even when they are amazing or "such an honor" or valuable—without letting other things go.

Not if we want to be creative. Not if we want to be okay. Not if we want to live fully. Not if we want to be our best selves.

I have the ability to keep going. To push through. To be strong, or appear strong, even when I am weak. Broken. Tired.

But I entered the summer season tired. Bone tired.

I began picturing myself in child's pose. Child's pose is a yoga posture for recovery that literally means *not doing* and *surrender*. I knew this was to be my posture for the coming months.

And so, I had to decide what I *wouldn't* do this summer ... even things that I had formerly enjoyed or that had been life-giving in the past.

I surrendered over-scheduling myself, being busy.

I surrendered my role as "cruise ship director" for my children. This was the summer of "make your own fun, kids!" (though yes, I still drove, and drove, and drove. And drove).

I surrendered planting flowers. I intentionally delayed planting my window boxes until our return from a family vacation at the end of June, because they would have died in our absence. But then, I never did plant them.

I surrendered gardening. For the first time in a decade, I didn't plant a vegetable garden.

I surrendered making jam.

I surrendered social media.

I surrendered participating in musical theater with our local theater company. Even though I felt like I was missing out. Even though I *was* missing out.

I surrendered chasing after social events and coffee dates.

I even surrendered writing. Or rather, writing for public consumption. I could never abandon my journal writing, lest I go insane.

I surrendered my need to know. I let go of *life as I have known it* and embraced all the uncertainty, all the discomfort, all the questions, and all the inconsistencies.

My *not-doing* (aka rest) involved behaviors I believed were restorative—choices that allowed me to maintain an inner posture of child's pose.

I rested with intense introversion. If you didn't hear from me this summer, please don't be offended or hurt. I had to be with myself. Obviously, with family and responsibilities, becoming a full-blown recluse was not in the cards. I saw the occasional friend or family member, but spent most of my time with my immediate family, or alone.

I rested with intentional silence and solitude. In Henri Nouwen's book, *The Way of the Heart*[1], he includes an illustration by Desert Father, Diadochus of Photiki:

> *"When the door of the steam bath is continually left open, the heat inside rapidly escapes through it; likewise, the soul, in its desire to say many things, dissipates its remembrance of God through the door of speech, even though everything it says may be good ... We have been made to believe that feelings, emotions and even inner stirrings of our souls have to be shared with others."*

I rested with mindfulness. In the past, I've been the implementer of my own meditation, but this summer I made use of simple apps like Headspace and Calm.[2]

I rested with reading. I read important, nourishing books that grew my brain. *And* I read ridiculous, fluffy novels that *for sure* diminished my intelligence (but were deliciously entertaining).

I rested with naps. Luxury, I know. Summers *"off"* allow for this. But don't be fooled, friends. We teachers work our twelve months in ten! Also, with teenagers, I can lay down for a few minutes and nobody dies. You'll get there, too, young mamas.

I rested with walks. Sometimes I walked for exercise. Sometimes for fresh air. Sometimes for the release of emotional angst or stress. Sometimes for thinking and listening.

I rested on the sunset deck almost every evening. I have a deck on the front of my house that overlooks the river. The sun sets on the hills, and if you walk or drive by our house, you'll often see me there. Probably with drinks. Probably with chips.

My summer of sabbatical was not about indulgence, but about healing. It was about unraveling my natural inclination to take care of everybody, to chase after people, to schedule myself to death, and to seek meaning and worth though *doing*. It has been about restricting energy flow to certain parts of my life so that other parts may thrive. It's been about making purposeful decisions about what I *do* and *don't do*.

And, as it turns out, I'm not finished yet. Though life has regained speed, my continued purpose is an inner posture of *surrender* and *not doing*. For how long, I'm not certain. The unraveling of everything has been remarkably alluring, and I'm compelled to continue on this path.

I'll write sometimes if I feel like it. Or I might take a nap instead.

Chapter 44

How To Save Your Own Life

"Gratitude unlocks the fullness of life. It turns what we have into enough, and more. It turns denial into acceptance, chaos to order, confusion to clarity. It can turn a meal into a feast, a house into a home, a stranger into a friend."

MELODY BEATTIE

It's a brand new year and we're all going to exercise more, complain less, call our grandmothers more, watch Netflix less, cook homemade meals more, and stop biting our nails … Bahahaha! Good luck with that. See you in a few weeks.

It's interesting to me that we lean so heavily on January 1st as a time to set goals, because really, *what is January 1st?* Our calendar is actually a fairly recent social construct.

Can you handle a brief history lesson? Our calendar as we know it, which is based on the Earth's solar rotations (years, months, days), with regular adjustments made for leap years and solstices, was only implemented in 1582 by Pope Gregory XIII. Most countries gradually adopted the Gregorian calendar as it was easier to follow than its predecessors, the lunar and Julian calendars. All of this to say, the manner by which we measure time is fairly new.

I typically see time as one continuous, unbroken passage, but within that timeline, I also envision a loopy line that makes room for the cycles that undoubtedly exist. Seasons, the phases of the moon, and even menstrual cycles are all circular loops embedded within the timeline. So, even though September is my *real* new year, and I'm aware that January 1st may or may not be the *actual* top of the year, I choose to use it as a stopping point for reflection. There is something sacred found in acknowledging and heeding the rhythms of life.

An uberly contemplative person, I find great meaning in the waning of one year and the dawning of the next. Though it's an arbitrary marker, I can almost feel the former draining away to make room for the new. And yearly, I accept the invitation to stop and ponder.

One of the yearly practices that guides my reflection involves asking and answering three simple questions: What was hard? What was great? What am I looking forward to?

I am an avid journaler; therefore, much of my life is documented in words—none of this new-fangled, online journal stuff—it's old school, hand-written words for me. I love my laptop, but when it comes to reflective writing, I'll take a pretty journal and a pen or pencil over a keyboard any day. My journal is not a diary, per se, documenting daily activity, though there can be some of that. It's a place of process and prayer. It records the sometimes extreme weather patterns of my emotions, and the wise, comforting words I hear back from my inner self and the voice of Love.

These physical records make it easy for me to read back through the pages, identifying highs and lows. Let me rephrase. It's easy to identify the highs and lows, *not* easy to read—it often feels pathetic and painful to read (gosh, I *reeeeally* feel things deeply!). This practice helps me to remember intentions I've set or what I've prayed and, often, to uncover those answers to prayer that may have been lost or unrealized amidst the daily grind. Reading through in one sitting also helps me to identify common threads and themes in my hopes and desires and also in how I've been led. Identifying and naming these reoccurring messages helps me to articulate my dreams and goals.

Even if you don't journal on a regular basis, or at all, take time to meander back through last year. Make room for pondering.

Begin with what was hard. I literally have the title "Things That Were Hard This Year" written and underlined at the top of a journal page. Very fancy indeed. I won't lie...this list can be tough. Many of us don't want to talk about the difficult things. We don't want to revisit the painful parts of the year. We don't want to focus on the negative. But acknowledging those darker shadow things is actually a pathway to wholeness and health. We're not going to stay there, we're simply going to say, "yeah, that sucked," and validate the experience.

Next, make a list of what was great. "Great" for me covers a wide swath of things and there are no rules. You get to decide what was a highlight, and, therefore, worth celebrating. Maybe a new baby in your family, a marriage, a new job. Perhaps you took a family vacation or received an award. Maybe your kid made the team or finally met some wonderful new friends. Maybe you saw Dave Matthews in concert. Maybe you renovated a bathroom. Maybe Jen Hatmaker followed you on Twitter (oh wait, that was a disappointing hoax. Scratch that). Maybe you learned to knit, or ski, or you got a tattoo. There are no qualifiers. If it was great for you, it goes on the list.

And finally, what are you looking forward to? For me, this typically combines resolution-esque ideas, practical and spiritual goals, as well as events I'm looking forward to during the upcoming year. Like everybody else, I'll probably plan to do more than *look* in the direction of my yoga mat. I'll likely cut out sugar again. I'd also like my clothes to continue fitting, but for someone who esteems good food and wine, this goal is lofty. Maybe I'll include "begin writing a book" or "have friends for dinner once a month." If we have a family vacation or event on the radar, I might note that as well.

I'm going to be brutally honest. Conjuring a list of things I'm looking forward to has been the hardest part of my practice this year. This 'year of our Lord' essentially took my hope into a back alley and kicked the shit out of it. So, naming hopes and dreams feels a little bit risky for me at the moment.

That being said, there were many amazing things in this last year and so much to be thankful for. One of the most monumental for me was that I finally summoned the courage to come out of the closet with my writing. My children are healthy, we have food on our table and God has stayed close by, even though I have had a year of holding my faith at arm's length. So, yes, there was a lot of good, but it was *also* really hard.

This one thing I know. No matter what else ends up on my list, there is one goal, above all other goals, that I'll continue to pursue. Every single day. No matter what.

It's the one resolution, the one goal, the one plan that makes the biggest difference. More than size 8 pants, more than writing a book, more than cutting out sugar, more than traveling to Costa Rica...

The one goal that will actually save your life is practicing gratitude.

If you want to change your life, look for what is good. Because if you're looking for the hard stuff, *you'll find it*. But if you're looking for the good stuff, *you'll find it*. When you change how you see, you change everything. Focusing on what is good doesn't make you an ostrich with your head in the sand. It doesn't make you delusional and out of touch with reality. It doesn't mean you deny or pretend that the hard stuff doesn't exist. It simply means that you decide what's in focus.

I do something called *"The Finger Thing"* with my students. It's a simple action that serves as a visual cue to better understand how to shift our focus:

Hold your index finger up in front of your nose, out far enough that you can see it without going cross-eyed. It should look like you're pointing to the sky or saying "we're #1!" Your finger in front of your face is the "hard thing." First, focus on the finger. You can still see everything else in the background, but it's blurred and out of focus. Now, keeping your finger in front of your face, shift your focus to the background and look around. As everything in the background becomes crisp and clear, the finger will be out of focus. The hard thing doesn't magically disappear (you can still see that it's there), but you're no longer giving it your sole attention.

What we hold in focus can easily determine our mood and energy. We can train ourselves to look beyond the hard thing and see all that is good. Be intentional. Write down why you are thankful every day. There are no rules; you are allowed to be thankful for whatever you want. My gratitude list is interspersed throughout my journal, but maybe you'll decide to use a designated list or book. It doesn't matter how you do it, just that you do.

In seasons of fulfillment, of plenty, and of dreams realized, stopping to say *thank you* is a celebration of joy. Gratitude flows easily. But in more trying times, when you're looking up from the bottom of the well, and you need Coke-bottle glasses to see the good—when your 'offering' is literally a *sacrifice* —gratitude will save your life.

I love the way that gratitude is described in this devotional reading by Sarah Young (you have to read it like Jesus is talking to you):

"Thankfulness takes the sting out of adversity. That is why I have instructed you to give thanks for everything. There is an element of mystery in this transaction: you give me thanks (regardless of your feelings), and I give you joy (regardless of your circumstances). This

is a spiritual act of obedience—at times, blind obedience. To people who don't know me intimately, it can seem irrational and even impossible to thank me for heartrending hardships. Nonetheless, those who obey me in this way are invariably blessed, even though difficulties may remain."[1]

Whatever hard thing is in your face right now, vying for (and even screaming for) your attention—financial difficulty, illness, rejection, job-loss, addiction, disappointment, loneliness, strained relationships, fear—I hope you'll pursue this one goal that will make the biggest difference. It might even save your life.

Live with gratitude.

Epilogue

A Door Of Hope

"Here is the world. Beautiful and terrible things will happen. Don't be afraid."

FREDERICK BUECHNER

I n times of transition, we may experience an ending, but lack insight pertaining to our next step. There may be nothing before us, or there may be so many options that we experience paralysis. For many months, *doorways* have been a recurring theme. Divine guidance, teaching and strategy for me during this time has been largely characterized by doors. Here's what I've learned thus far:

"There are things known and unknown, and in between are the doors." [1] (Jim Morrison)

The dictionary says doors are hinged, sliding, or revolving barriers at the entrance to buildings, rooms, vehicles, and cupboards. But doorways aren't only barricades, they are also transitions between spaces. Though they may represent an ending or a leaving, they equally represent a beginning or an arrival. Just as doors are entrances and exits in the physical, they also have symbolism in the spiritual.

This year has been filled with widespread change for me, where I have transitioned (or am transitioning) from long term work positions and life situations that have been meaningful and life-giving toward new endeavours. The process has involved a long period of sensing change and wrongly identifying what it might relate to *about four. million. times.* I have experienced a funnel-like narrowing down from the unknown to the known.

"If it doesn't open, it's not your door." [2] (Unknown)

This season of too many choices and unknowns appeared before me like a long hotel corridor, with doors lining both sides of the hallway at regular intervals. This part required action and agency. I had no idea where to begin or which doors were for me, but I sensed a prompting to turn knobs, to rattle doors, and bang hard to see if any would open. If a door remained closed, I proceeded to the next, applying all of the same techniques. I worked my way down the corridor, weaving from one side to the other, until finally, a door swung open. It was clearly the one open to me, so I walked through.

It was tempting to feel discouraged at various points when a door wouldn't budge. But I determined *not* to look at each closed door as failure, but as an indication that it was not the right thing. The closed door was not rejection, it was guidance to keep moving forward.

"A very little key will open a very heavy door." [3] (Charles Dickens)

The next phase of my door experience involved something akin to storming the castle gates. Sometimes a closed door is a hard no, but occasionally, there are imposed barricades that *need* to be conquered and broken down. You may not have beheld an actual battering ram in my arms, but in unseen realms, I was applying all of the forces at my disposal—in other words, setting an intention, or prayer.

I believe strongly in the power of our thoughts, intentions, and/ or prayer. I'm not talking about a wimpy *"now I lay me down to sleep"* recitation or a passive, memorized script, spouted with little to no thought. Prayer is truly a little key that will open heavy doors.

It is a powerful aligning of our spirit with divine Love. It's an active and vocal declaration. It's knowing our strength and authority, and raising our voices and swords. During this phase, I fasted, prayed, and wielded my sword. You might have mistaken me for a tired girl on a sofa, but if you'd put on your spiritual glasses, you'd have seen Wonder Woman, complete with cuffs and crown.

"The doors of opportunity often swing on the hinges of opposition!" [4] (Adrian Rogers)

The next door analogy was a picture of two very different structures before me. One was a large, arched doorway, made of wood and iron, so enormous it made me feel like shrunken Alice. It was the sort you'd imagine in a castle wall. The other was an odd-looking doorway in the shape of a cross. It reminded me of a painting done by my good friend David Hayward (you may know him as the nakedpastor) many years ago called *Narrow Way.*[5]

Though the grand looking door would have been easier to pass through, I knew I was to enter the narrow door. The accompanying message was *"just because something is easy doesn't mean it is right, just as something that's difficult to navigate doesn't mean that it's wrong."* In this case, I had to twist and contort my body in order to fit through the doorway. It wasn't straightforward. It was mildly uncomfortable. I definitely felt the opposition. But it was right.

"There I will give her back her vineyards and will make the Valley of Achor a door of hope." [6] **(Hosea 2.15)**

The last phase of my door-dom learning experience has been one of immense excitement and joy. I wrote something in my journal that I felt God was saying to me. I sensed I would be receiving new instructions, and that I needed to be listening and prepared to act, to be watching and ready to *walk through*. I felt I was to follow gut urges and to pay attention to what I thought were my own crazy ideas. I was instructed not to write them off but to write them down.

The last months have been crazy and wonderful. After all of the doorknob-rattling, gate-storming and contorting, something changed. The words *"door of hope"* played on repeat in my mind. After months of hard terrain in the valley of Achor (which translates to "the valley of trouble"), open doors began appearing before me, almost like sci-fi portals to other realms. As I have trusted and walked through them, I have found myself transported. There has been a sense of ease, and peace, and rightness that has brought so much joy and solace.

It's miraculous to me that something that began as a massive unknown has been formed and shaped and refined into the most beautiful thing. What began as an overwhelming amount of doors—most locked, barricaded, and useless—has been narrowed down to the one right thing.

Yes, it felt overwhelming. Yes, it took some time. Yes, it required trust and confidence. But now, I find myself on the threshold of new adventure that fulfills more promises in one fell swoop than I could possibly have believed.

Be encouraged. Love *does* do immeasurably more than we could ask for or imagine.[7]

Thank you for braving this vulnerable, necessary, courageous journey, my friend. It's been an honor to walk with you.

Notes

Chapter 2: Opting For Uncomfortable

1. Anonymous; has been attributed to numerous people

Chapter 3: Holding On For Dear Life

1. Jesus, John 16:33 NRSV

2. Saint Patrick, "Saint Patrick's Breastplate," Liber Hymnorum

Chapter 4: No One, No Thing

1. C.S. Lewis, paraphrasing Augustine

Chapter 7: Not Dead

1. Romans 4:17 NRSV

2. John 11:25 NRSV

Chapter 8: Tapestry

1. Terry Leblanc, speaking at National Vineyard Gathering, Penticton, BC. July 2010

Chapter 10: Deadhead

1. For more information on the Enneagram, search enneagraminstitute.com, or read *The Road Back To You* by Ian Cron and Suzanne Stabile, 2016

Chapter 13: Crashing Waves

1. Elisabeth Kubler-Ross, first in *On Death and Dying* 1969

Chapter 19: Forgive Me?

1. Wikipedia, en.wikipedia.org

2. "The Lord's Prayer," Matthew 6:9-13 NRSV

3. Karen Swartz, MD, The John Hopkins Hospital, hopkinsmedecine.org/health/wellness-and-prevention/forgiveness-you-health-depends-on-it

Chapter 23: Au revoir, Joy-Thief

1. For more information, search "research between social media use and anxiety."

Chapter 25: You Are Not The Only One

1. Maya Angelou, Oprah's Master Class appearance

Chapter27: Fully You

1. Gord Downey, "Ahead By A Century," The Tragically Hip, 1996

2. Marianne Williamson, *A Return To Love: Reflections on the Principles of a Course in Miracles*, 1992

3. Brené Brown, "The Power of Vulnerability", www.ted.com/talks/brene_brown_the_power_of _vulnerability

Chapter 29: Speak Up

1. Quote by Edmund Burke

Chapter 34: Lean Hard

1. Elisabeth Kübler-Ross, David Kessler, *Life Lessons: Two Experts on Death and Dying Teach Us About the Mysteries of Life and Living*, 2000

2. C.S. Lewis, *Letters to Malcolm: Chiefly on Prayer*, 1964

Chapter 37: Does Everyone Have Friends But Me?

1. Julia Cameron, *The Artist's Way*, 1992

Chapter 38: Telephone-Pole-To-Telephone-Pole

1. Gertrude Stein, *Everybody's Autobiography*, 1937

2. Ann Voskamp, *One Thousand Gifts*, 2011

Chapter 39: Keeping It Real IV

1. Jack Handey, "Deep Thoughts," Saturday Night Live

Chapter 41: A Nasty Case Of The Februarys

1. Julian of Norwich, 1343-1416

Chapter 42: Autumnal Reflections: What Needs To Go?

1. Ecclesiastes 3:1-8 NRSV

Chapter 43: Sabbatical

1. Diadochus of Photiki, quoted by Henri Nouwen, *The Way of the Heart*, 1981

2. "Headspace" and "Calm" are both available for trial or purchase in your App Store.

Chapter 44: How To Save Your Own Life

1. Sarah Young, *Jesus Calling*

Epilogue: A Door of Hope

1. Quote by Jim Morrison

2. Quote by Unknown

3. Quote by Charles Dickens

4. Quote by Adrian Rogers

5. "The Narrow Way", painting by David Hayward, aka the nakedpastor

6. Hosea 2:15 NRSV

7. Ephesians, 3:2 NRSV

About the Author

Ellen is a family-prioritizing, coffee-drinking, truth-telling, authenticity-pursuing, list-making, God-seeking, world-loving, ambiverted, wine-imbibing, question-asking, former closet writer. She's a traveller and an educator. Ellen was a worship leader at many churches and conferences for years, and was a song-writer and singer on several albums. The words "laid back" have never been used to describe her. She is spicy, empathetic, and honest. She is an unabashed over-user of hashtags and emojis. The message written on Ellen's heart is one of identity; she is passionate about living authentically as the person she was created to be and helping others to do likewise.

Ellen lives on the east coast of Canada with her family. She calls her teenagers "occasionally mind-boggling, and entirely magnificent." In addition to writing, she teaches French to High School students... and all remaining hours are, quite literally, spent in her vehicle, driving the teenagers to hockey practices, rehearsals, horseback riding, and to visit friends. It's a full, imperfect and magnificent life.

She can be found at:

- www.ellencompton.com
- Instagram @ _ellencompton_
- Facebook @Ellen Compton

For more information about Ellen Compton,
or to contact her for speaking engagements,
please visit *www.EllenCompton.com*

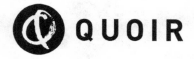

Many voices. One message.

Quoir is a boutique publisher
with a singular message: *Christ is all.*
Venture beyond your boundaries to discover Christ
in ways you never thought possible.

For more information, please visit
www.quoir.com